A TIMELY GUIDE TO
SHARING JESUS

LET GOD SPEAK

A TIMELESS METHOD FOR
SHARING JESUS

LET GOD
SPEAK

"David Collum's *Let God Speak* is an honest, earnest, and practical guide for motivating all of us non-evangelists to do the work of evangelism. His leadership of The Pocket Testament League enables countless copies of the Gospel of John to be lovingly given around the globe in a multitude of languages. I am grateful for his impact on my life and the outreach of Westminster Seminary in Philadelphia. Read this clear call for faithful witness and discover the joy of sharing gospel hope through the written word of our sovereign God with the divine appointments he deigns to place in our daily paths."

—**PETER A. LILLBACK**, President, Westminster Theological Seminary, Philadelphia

"David helps the potentially zealous, frustrated, or stuck Christian with 'good news' about the Good News: there is a realistic way to begin truly following Jesus without all of the imagined pressure. What if getting out of the way and letting God speak was the key to getting in the game? So simple and real it might just work!"

—**MIKE SHARROW**, CEO, C12 Business Forums, San Antonio

"In *Let God Speak*, David Collum gives us good news for evangelism. Packed with personal testimonies and centered in God's Word, *Let God Speak* moves the follower of Jesus into the liberating reality that God himself is at the center of our evangelism. When we seek Him, we are engaging with Him. Collum draws on his significant experience and offers the reader confidence in sharing the Christian faith with other people."

—**THE RT. REV. JULIAN M DOBBS**, Diocesan Bishop, Anglican Diocese of the Living Word, Virginia

A TIMELESS METHOD FOR
SHARING JESUS

LET GOD SPEAK

DAVID COLLUM

HIGH BRIDGE BOOKS
HOUSTON

Let God Speak
by David Collum

Copyright © 2022 David Collum

All rights reserved.

Printed in the United States of America
ISBN: 978-1-954943-52-0

All rights reserved. Except in the case of brief quotations embodied in critical articles and reviews, no portion of this book may be reproduced, stored in a retrieval system, or transmitted in any form or by any means—electronic, mechanical, photocopy, recording, scanning, or other—without prior written permission from the author.

Unless otherwise noted, Scripture quotations are the The Holy Bible, World English Bible (WEB) and is in the public domain.

High Bridge Books titles may be purchased in bulk for educational, business, fundraising, or sales promotional use. For information, please contact High Bridge Books via www.HighBridgeBooks.com/contact.

Read-Carry-Share ® is a registered trademark of The Pocket Testament League and used with permission.

Published in Houston, Texas, by High Bridge Books.

To The Pocket Testament League Board of Directors and Members, and to Michael Brickley, past President of The League, who took a step of faith in allowing me to be a part of such a great organization and learn the Power of God's Word.

INTRODUCTION

I love Jesus. I want everyone to meet Jesus. Jesus' love for me, his rescue of me by giving his own life—compels me.

I love to read books and learn how to tell people about Jesus. I read a lot of them. From Michael Green's massive 600-page *Evangelism Through the Local Church,* to David Kinnaman's convicting work *un-Christian,* to Bill Hybel's intimate invitation *Just Walk Across the Room,* to Bill Bright's concise 16-page book *Have You Heard of the Four Spiritual Laws,* they, and many others, are chock full of deep insights, new methods, and the latest trends. The problem is putting all this head knowledge into action. I have always struggled to do it.

And I'm a pastor.

As a pastor, the pulpit actually provided me a false sense of protection. Each week I labored to present the Gospel. I knew many in the church may not have a saving relationship with Jesus. Therefore, I worked hard on my preaching on Sunday and during our weekly Bible Studies. I took comfort that I was doing evangelism.

I would tell myself I was:

- Not that "guy on the corner yelling at people with a bullhorn."

- Not that "guy in the elevator who turns, faces you, and asks, "If the elevator cable snapped and we plummeted to our death in the next 15 seconds, do you know where you are going?""

- Not that "guy offering comments to a stranger, thinking his comments are helpful, but in reality, is just one more Christian committing all the sins of insensitivity the church is forever guilty of."

I was thoughtful, well-read, ready to answer objections, and on good days even a bit winsome.

To be clear, I was doing evangelism. The problem was I rarely looked a single person in the eye while I did it.

Then, the Lord brought me to a new season, a season out of the pulpit. I miss the pulpit. I miss the Bible Studies. I miss the people. I miss them terribly.

But God had a huge gift for me—and I want to share this gift with you.

I won't wrap this gift in the latest research. I won't give you the prevailing (and intimidating) attitudes of the world. I won't dazzle and depress you with statistics. I won't remind you of all the things the church, and maybe you, have done wrong.

Nope, I won't do those things.

Why? Because I realized, at least for me, that while all those things are true, they parallelized me. I essentially would convince myself I was not gifted in the area of sharing my faith. Not one-to-one, at least.

What God has now shown me is a way to let Him lead, to have me actually look at people, and to realize He has provided something far more powerful than my words. What's even more cool is that in the end, I actually now see people as people!

I would love to share this gift with you—let's get started.

1

THE IMPERATIVE

im·per·a·tive[1]
/əmˈperədiv/

adjective

1. of vital importance; crucial.
   "immediate action was imperative"

2. giving an authoritative command; peremptory.
   "the bell pealed again, a final imperative call"

"Go & Make": Don't Confuse Simple with Easy

This book is about Jesus' command from Matthew 28:19, to "go & make." Ever notice Jesus' commands are mostly one-syllable words? Love, Serve, Obey, Go, Make. Interesting. What do you take away from Jesus' commands? I take away two points.

First, Jesus' commands are commands of both action and urgency. They require us to expend energy. They seem anything but optional. I hear the imperative in his voice.

Second, Jesus' commands are *simple* to comprehend. However, don't confuse *simple* with *easy*.

Many parts of our existence can be lived by following uncomplicated, simple, yet hard to practice day-in and day-out, principles or rules.

Consider the following *simple* situations. Want to lose weight? It's simple! Eat fewer calories than you consume. Want to stop smoking? It's simple! Ween your body off nicotine. It should only take 20+ days for the nicotine to be out of your body. Want to understand time travel? It is simple — $E = mc^2$.

While we may all know those above statements, and we may even be able to write Einstein's Theory of Special Relativity, we would no doubt not use the word *easy* to describe any of them.

Two observations. First, we are the benefactors of the originator's hard work of developing and testing the above theories. Second, while they may roll off our tongues, they can be difficult to accept and even more difficult to master.

My point? Simple does not equal easy. The simple statements above are true. In reality, losing weight, no longer being tormented by the craving for a cigarette, and understanding Einstein's Theory of Relativity are far from easy. Further, we would never even dream of claiming that these three examples were easy to carry out.

However, so often I find in the Church that as we admonish ourselves for not following Jesus' simple commands, we do so in a way that implies they should be easy to carry out. Consider an earlier cited book, *Just Walk Across the Room*. What do you hear in that title? Perhaps it is just my ears, but I hear that it should be easy.

Yes, Jesus' direction is never complicated. Yes, his commands are simple to understand. Unlike Einstein's Theories, no PhD is required. However, these easily comprehensible commands are not easy to perform. Just like Nike's *Just Do It*, drive and determination are needed.

Many through the centuries have possessed the needed drive to carry out Jesus' simple, straightforward direction. Yet in our desire to fulfill the Master's commands, we, at times, have either given up because of frustration and failure or complicated his direction.

Yes, in our drive to obey, we can complicate and overthink Jesus' command about how to go about sharing our faith. Consider a parallel situation in the Bible. Do you remember Jesus' teaching about loving your neighbor in Luke 10:25-37? As Jesus points his questioners back to God's Word about loving your neighbor, he is asked, "Who is my neighbor?" The text says that the person asking that question was seeking to justify himself. I understand this to mean that if they can tightly define "neighbor" as a small group, in fact the smallest possible group, then they have a chance at fulfilling the Law. They might just be successful.

I don't often think I am like the person in Luke's Gospel. I don't think I am trying to justify myself. Yet, if I am honest, I want to be successful in following Jesus—without having to leave my comfort zone. In reality, I am very similar to the person asking the question.

Might this be true of most of us? As Christians, we want to feel like we are following Jesus. There is, however, a trap. Our need for success, our need to justify to ourselves that we are good Christians, nullifies God's love toward us. We forget that God loves us unconditionally. We turn inward, trying to prove to ourselves, to justify to ourselves, that we are worthy of His love.

Without realizing it, we have turned inside-out a very simple to understand command: love your neighbor. That inside-outness has another consequence. We become legalistic. We essentially say, "I will fulfill the Law, but not go one iota further!" We've taken a simple command and now are not only not doing it, but we are also limiting ourselves.

Consider that when we love our neighbor (as when we share our faith) in addition to blessing them, we are blessed. We grow.

We become more like Jesus. Jesus' only had one, you might say, limit. Full obedience to His Father. Jesus tells us in John 15:9-11 that he desires that we love him as he loved the Father. When we limit our obedience to Jesus, we limit our growth. We shrink our view of what God can do in us.

Limited growth is not the only consequence. Our failure in living these commands day-in and day-out frustrates us. The more we are lectured about them, the more the frustration builds. We look for an escape from this guilt. We look for someone else to assign responsibility to carry them out. We find refuge in a number of places.

One place is in the idea of Spiritual Gifts. We take comfort in assigning ourselves into a category of "not my spiritual gift." We might not realize it, but we have become like the person asking, "Who is my neighbor?" If he can identify someone as "not his neighbor," then he is freed of responsibility. If we can identify that God did not give us the "gift" of evangelism, then we too can be freed of the responsibility to "go & make." We, now standing outside the problem, can offer criticism without injury to ourselves. We simply criticize those "responsible."

We have moved from complicating Jesus' direction to criticizing others who are not living it. Hang around a few of us church folks and the criticism rolls off our tongues about how the church is not "going and making." And hey, people are right to criticize, but I think Jesus has said something about this in Matthew 7:5, having to do with eyes and beams/planks.

By now, you've grasped that a huge chasm exists between simple and easy. For the church, for followers of Jesus, there is more.

Obeying God is a spiritual battle!

The Bible teaches us that receiving Jesus into our hearts is not the finish line. No, it is the starting line of a new life, a new journey.

We start living a life devoted to God. We will wrestle along the path of this journey. That wrestling is not against flesh and blood, but as it says in Ephesians 6:12, against spiritual forces.

Anytime we seek to order our lives around God's principles, we face spiritual opposition. Opposition from the enemy comes in many forms, from the subtle to the direct. We can be distracted from the specific principle we are trying to obey, even distracted to apparently other good deeds. Consider how we might tell ourselves that because we are feeding the hungry, we need not obey Jesus' command to "go & make." Beyond distraction, we can become discouraged when we try and do not see the results we want to see. We can become angry when others criticize us. We can, in many places around the world, be beaten or worse, as we seek to obey. All of this is from the enemy.

All issues in our lives are "spiritual battles." We need to remind ourselves that God's principles apply not merely to what the world labels as spiritual or religious. God owns all of it and all of us! What we eat and drink. How we work. How we talk. All of this is to be devoted to Him.

When we seek to live our lives by following God's commands, as Arthur Conan Doyle's character Sherlock Holmes would say, "the game is afoot." However, this "game" is deadly serious, for we are battling with Satan. Let's simply list the seven deadly sins: greed, lust, envy, gluttony, wrath, sloth, and pride. Please note that not sharing your faith isn't on the list. The list is full of the everyday activities of life. Satan twists, fills these with lies, and turns our using them wrongly into sin. Food gets twisted to gluttony. Rest gets twisted to sloth. The list goes on. The Father of Lies is a master twister. And Satan's aim is to twist all of life.

Now imagine you want to "go & make."

For Satan, you have now entered into full-on battle. Charles Alexander, co-founder of The Pocket Testament League, said, "The last thing the devil will let you do is win a soul definitely to Christ. If you don't believe it, try it. He will let you never miss a prayer meeting or Sunday service; he will even let you get up and lecture on religious subjects, and do all sorts of religious deeds, if you will stop short of one thing—get face-to-face with individuals, to bring them to a decision for Jesus Christ, and to get them to confess Him openly before the world."[2] Charles should know; he spent his life seeking to win souls.

When we choose to try and win souls, Satan goes to work. He will use any part of our lives to get us twisted and turned, and thereby sideline us from living out Jesus' simple, straightforward command.

You might think, given that eternity is at stake, God would have a different plan.

There Is No Plan B

There is this old joke.[3] Jesus has just risen from the dead and ascended to heaven. He is hanging out with some angels on the clouds. They are looking down upon the earth. One angel says, "Lord, that was amazing; we thought you were a "goner." We thought it was over. But then, you rose from the dead. You trampled death under your feet. You've defeated Satan! What's next?" Jesus answered, "I left a handful of people who really believe in me, and they will tell the world about me and make disciples."

The angels were stunned. They simply stared at Jesus. The silence got to the point of being uncomfortable. Finally, one angel tentatively asked, "Lord, what is Plan B?"

Jesus answered, "There is no Plan B."

Funny? Sort of. But if the eternal destiny of God's children is at stake, then two reactions seem to happen inside of us.

- First, we immediately understand how terribly important this assignment from God is, and in our minds, nothing short of perfection will do.
- Second, because we fall woefully short of perfection, in addition to the frustration and criticism we succumb to (described earlier), we spend energy asking, "Why would God the Father build this sort of plan, a plan that depends on us?"

Let's spend some time looking at the question, "Why would God build this sort of a plan?" Answering this question first requires caution. I am trying to explain God's reasoning. He certainly owes us no such explanation. He is the Almighty.

Further, to seek to explain God could be rightly viewed as arrogant. For me, setting off to do so brings God's booming voice from the Book of Job to mind. Listen to God speak in Job 38:4, "Were you there when I laid the foundations of the world, declare if you have understanding..." God continues his discourse through chapter 38, then chapter 39, and chapter 40 of the Book of Job. Job's response? He replied, not with words, but by simply putting his hand over his mouth. In many ways, I feel as if I should put my hand over my mouth.

I want, however, to press into this question because I believe it might yield insight and learning for us as we seek to "go & make."

I asked above, "Why would God the Father..." I chose this parental language for a specific reason. Jesus describes our relationship to the Almighty as filial. We are his children. He, a perfect parent. Parents often take specific approaches with their children for their offspring's long-term good.

I believe God's approach is very much like raising children. He seeks to raise us up into spiritual adulthood. His motive is love. The challenge for me to understand this as the answer is rooted in my concept of God as love. Do I, do we, have a right understanding of love?

C.S. Lewis writes about this in *The Problem of Pain* using the language of family.

> We want, in fact, not so much a Father in Heaven as a grandfather in heaven—a senile benevolence who, as they say, "liked to see young people enjoying themselves" and whose plan for the universe was simply that it might be truly said the end of each day, "a good time was had by all." Not many people, I admit, would formulate a theology in precisely those terms: but a conception not very different lurks at the back of many minds. I do not claim to be an exception: I should very much like to live in a universe which was governed on such lines. *But since it is abundantly clear that I don't, and since I have reason to believe, nevertheless, that, God is Love, I conclude that my conception of love needs correction.*
>
> I might, indeed, have learned, even from the poets, that Love is something more stern and splendid than mere kindness: that even the love between the sexes is, as in Dante, 'a lord of terrible aspect.' There is kindness in Love: but *Love and kindness are not coterminous, and when kindness (in the sense given above) is separated from the other elements of Love, it involves a certain fundamental indifference to its object,* and even something like contempt of it. Kindness consents very readily to the removal of its object – we have all met people whose kindness to animals is constantly leading them to kill animals lest they should suffer. *Kindness, merely as such, cares not whether its object becomes good or bad, provided only that it escapes suffering.* As Scripture points out, it is bastards who are spoiled: the legitimate sons, who are to carry on the family tradition, are punished (Hebrews 12:8). It is for people whom we care nothing about that we

> demand happiness on any terms: with our friends, our lovers, our children, we are exacting and would rather see them suffer much than be happy in contemptible and estranging modes. If God is Love, He is, by definition, something more than mere kindness. And it appears, from all the records, that though He has often rebuked us and condemned us, He has never regarded us with contempt. He has paid us the intolerable compliment of loving us, in the deepest, most tragic, most inexorable sense.[4]

C.S. Lewis, as always, writes in a way where a small snippet is chockfull of ideas to consider. His point that love and kindness are not coterminous is the path to understanding our question as to why God's Plan of having humans "go & make" is his Plan A.

At first pass, we might not understand God's Plan as the best plan. Our visceral reaction that God should have a better plan is largely driven by our desire that everyone would turn to Jesus. It is wonderful that our hearts beat with this longing that all the world know Jesus. As we think about evangelism, we immediately realize so many have not heard the Name of Jesus. The burden we feel for those yet to meet him naturally makes us feel inadequate, knowing how much further we have to go to get better at sharing our faith.

We have the Father's heart in us, for we, like he, desire none should perish (2 Peter 3:9).

Yet the Father also has a heart for us. He wants us to become sons and daughters. Returning to C.S. Lewis' quote, God is interested in more than being kind to us. He is interested in loving us. His love encourages us to obey, and through obedience, we become more and more sons and daughters. In the end, he cares about being in relationship with us.

And so the race is on, the race to follow Jesus, to obey and to love God. We look for reasons and for help. We want our behavior to come into accord with God's simple instructions. We then make a mistake. We have this belief that if we could simply understand all the reasons behind God's decisions, laws, etc., then we could more easily fulfill them.

I want to dissuade us from chasing that trail. Running down that rabbit hole simply confuses us. Point of fact: Understanding the simple principle behind a law does not make following that law easy.

Consider this example from Genesis chapters one through three. In the beginning, God creates the world. God creates Adam and Eve in His image. Everything is perfect. God walks with Adam and Eve in the cool of the evening. God tells and explains that they can have all but one thing. There is one tree they cannot eat from. He did not have to tell them why, but he does. He tells them if they eat of its fruit, they will die.

Pause and reflect for a moment. God gives them a straightforward and simple singular command. He does not stop there. God gives them a straightforward and simple explanation. If they eat from the tree, they will die. Furthermore, he has given them everything else save for this one tree.

Yet, even with the reason for the rule, they cannot comply. They are not alone in this scene. We so often, when we think about this scene, think in purely human, almost secular, terms. However, everything in life has a spiritual dimension. In this scene are not merely Adam and Eve, but Satan and God.

God is not powerless. Quite far from it. Yet Adam and Eve succumb to the temptation. They had one simple command. Don't eat the fruit from one tree. They eat. Sin, and its fruit, death, enter the world.

I bring up the Creation and Fall stories not only to reinforce that *simple* is not *easy*. I bring it up to introduce one other point by asking, "Was Jesus' Plan B to a failed attempt by God in the Garden of Eden to create a perfect world?"

No, it was not a failed attempt! The plan to send God the Son to die the most excruciating death of all time was God's Plan before the foundations of the world were laid (1 Peter 1:18-20).

Jesus is Plan A. So too are we God's Plan A to "go & make." Sometimes God's Plan A is hard for us to understand.

I took us through this long bit of C.S. Lewis and the creation story to answer "one question and make one point." Remember the question?

> Why would God the Father build a plan for the redemption of the world that depends on us telling everyone about Jesus?

The answer is God does not depend on us. He did not plan or depend on Adam and Eve obeying. He no more depends on us to perfectly perform in order for His Will to succeed.

We confuse the aim of our Creator's calculus. We believe that "go & make" is singularly about all non-believers becoming believers through our labors. God's plan to have you and me "go & make," to tell the entire world about Jesus, is as much about you and me becoming his followers, his disciples, as it is evangelism. It is as much about our growth as sons and daughters as anything else!

Our life of faith is always two-sided. Evangelism on one side and Discipleship on the other. By "two-sided," I mean that our coming to Jesus, our being drawn to him, is the Good News coming to us—we have been evangelized. Yet God's work, God's love, does not stop there. Once evangelized, we begin the lifelong journey of following Jesus. We are now on the path of discipleship (a part of which includes evangelizing others). Thanks be to God that He is literally inside of us, you might say in between these two outwardly facing parts of our lives.

His Plan is, in fact, perfectly good. Since Jesus' ascension, billions have gone and made disciples, and billions more have come to know Jesus as Lord.

God's plan, of which he is completely sovereign, is nothing short of a brilliantly elegant equation that simultaneously turns babes of the faith into sons and daughters, all while new babes are born—who in turn "go & make."

Be secure in God's sovereignty. We must free our minds from this idea that God's plan depends on our perfection. We can "go & make," replacing guilt with freedom and hope and joy because our confidence is shifted from ourselves "to Him who is able to do exceedingly abundantly above all than we ask or think" (Ephesians 3:20).

All of these thoughts bring me back not only to the importance but the urgency of inviting others to meet Jesus.

We Are Always Just One Generation Away

This is why, I believe, God has arranged the passing of faith as if it is always just one generation away from being lost. Because what is lost is not only people coming to faith but those who have faith, losing theirs because it slowly evaporates from inaction.

To reiterate, this does not mean that we can somehow thwart God's plan of redemption for His World. We cannot. The Bible chronicles times when God's people seemingly petered away, and He intervened.

Genesis 6, the story of Noah, is one such time. We read in verse 5, "Yahweh saw that the wickedness of man was great in the earth, and that every imagination of the thoughts of man's heart was continually only evil." Noah and his small family seemed to be the only ones following God.

Yet from Noah sprung Abraham! God is not thwarted. Even after Abraham's great-grandson was thrown into a well and left for dead, God was not thwarted. Even after Israel sought a human king more than God, his plans were not thwarted. Even after that earthly kingdom over and over abandoned the Law, God was not thwarted. Even after Jesus was nailed to a cross, God was not thwarted – in fact, God was in control the entire time.

God is in control on a cosmic, earthly, and personal level. Yes, as humans, we make it much harder than we need to when we turn away from him. We make it harder when we turn away from Him as individuals, as families, as churches, as villages and towns, as states, and as nations.

This is why "go & make" is so important, not just to those who have yet to hear the name of Jesus, but to those who have.

When you hear the command "go & make," perhaps your reaction is to get defensive (that had been my reaction). Let me encourage you not to proclaim that you don't have the gift (another of my reactions). When you hear there is No Plan B, don't freak out that God is laying some heavy guilt on you. When you hear we are always one generation away from losing the faith, don't despair. Think of Adam and Eve, and Noah, and all the other men and women of the Bible that when they were overwhelmed, God provided.

With this perspective of God, there is no need to despair. Instead, we can get in the game, the game of Evangelism—with confidence.

You might be questioning the word "confidence." You might be thinking, "I can't!" Yet my encouragement to have confidence comes not from human wisdom but from God. Here is what God says in Philippians 1:6: "…being confident of this very thing, that He who began a good work in you will complete it until the day of Christ Jesus." Who is this "He"? None other than Jesus. What is this "good work"? None other than becoming a son or daughter.

Take one more step with me. Free of all those overwhelming feelings just described, let's press in and think a little more about each of us sharing our faith. Evangelism might not be natural for you. In chapter two, we will go beyond the urgency to share our faith and explore the benefits and the joy when we do invite others to consider Jesus. Then in chapters three and four, we will get practical, sharing a simple, repeatable method that anyone can do.

[1] Definition from Oxford Languages and Google, languages.oup.com/google-dictionary-en/, accessed May 1, 2022.

[2] Helen Cadbury, *Charles Alexander, A Romance of Song and Soul-Winning. By His Wife* (Originally published Marshall Brothers. London. Republished by Forgotten Books. 2012), p. 12.

[3] Joe Aldrich, *Lifestyle Evangelism: Learning to Open Your Life to Those Around You* (Portland, OR.: Multnomah Press. 2006), pp. 15-16.

[4] C.S. Lewis, *The Problem of Pain. The Complete C.S. Lewis Signature Classics* (Harper One. New York. 2002), p. 567.

2

EVANGELISM, WHO ME?

e·van·ge·lism[1]
/əˈvanjəˌlizəm/

noun

1. the spreading of the Christian gospel by public preaching or personal witness.
    a. zealous advocacy of a cause.
       "I arrived in a state of high evangelism"

The Need for Personal Work

As noted, God does not need us to do His work of redeeming His good creation. He lets us help him. He, in fact, uses this work as much to build us up as his followers as to reach those who have yet to hear his name.

People do the work of sharing their faith in many different ways. Some methods appear big and bold, such as when we see the evangelist on stage in front of thousands. Other methods seem to appear laser-like, such as when we observe the person involved in a debate demonstrating not only their intellect but their agility to handle multiple arguments, all the while never losing the aim of presenting Jesus. Still other methods, such as feeding the hungry and serving those in need, overflow with compassion. This work of evangelism, while it shares a common goal, is truly varied in its methods. My bookshelves are filled with books on the methods of evangelism just highlighted, with even more books highlighting still more ways to reach people for Christ.

I expect most of those methods have proven results. I love the creativity of all the varied ways. I love the passion. I must tell you, many of those ways don't fit me.

Yet I am convinced, as put forth in chapter one, that we need to do evangelism as much for ourselves as for those we are trying to reach. For those of us for whom these ways don't fit, what can we do?

I want to begin to unpack something called Personal Work, and our need for it. Personal Work is the work we do, as a follower of Jesus, in reaching out to another person in love, to invite them to consider the person of Jesus as God and Savior.

In chapters three and four, I will propose one straightforward, time-tested method of Personal Work. However, let me first unpack this idea.

Personal Work is first and foremost you and me, individually or in a small group, "going." We are going to another person, or possibly a small group. Personal Work is when we look at a person, face-to-face, and invite them to consider Jesus. We do this with a motivation of love. When we are face-to-face, our intentions are immediately obvious. Do we see the humanity in the person? Does our genuine concern for them show through? Or are we more enamored with ourselves, seeing them as another possible "notch on our belt" of conversions?

Here is where we get a glimpse of Jesus. We have so many stories of him being face-to-face. The woman at the well, the synchro-Phoenician woman begging him, Jairus, the unnamed woman with the blood disorder, Martha, Mary, Lazarus…the list goes on. In each instance, Jesus meets those people right where they are.

Our "going" has the specific purpose of inviting them to meet Jesus. To be sure, people "go" with other purposes in mind. Many wonderful acts of mercy are done in the world. Fewer of those works extend a real invitation to the Savior. Personal Work may be done amid works of mercy, but those works of mercy always expressly invite someone to consider Jesus.

Now, as you read this, you might not be doing evangelism. If so, your natural reaction might be a sigh, frustration, or even defensiveness. If so, perhaps your reaction is because you have had experiences where Christians or the Church heaped guilt on you for not sharing your faith. If you are feeling this way, hold off putting this book down.

Before you get frustrated by this direct push and before you say to me (and yourself), "I am not an evangelist, I don't have that spiritual gift," let me tell you that in the chapters that follow, I lay out the great news about how *simple* (not easy) it is.

Why am I encouraging you to keep reading? I know the feelings many of us have when we feel like we are being lectured about evangelism. I am one late to this world of Personal Work.

For now, if you feel the guilt, just rebuke Satan. Last time I checked in Galatians 5, guilt is not a fruit of the Spirit. Further, you might need to push away from your mind bad experiences you've had as you consider this idea. The idea that it might become one of the great blessings of your life.

Billy Graham, a giant in the world of large-scale evangelism, taught that Personal Work was the best way of reaching people.[2] In other words, Graham would say we "need" to do this work in order to "go & make."

I have thought about Graham, this giant of evangelism, and his comment a great deal. I add to Graham's assertion Charles and Helen Alexander's similar point of view.

Unlike Billy Graham, you probably don't know what Charles Alexander and his wife Helen Cadbury Alexander spent much of their energy on. They are the founders of The Pocket Testament League. Helen started The Pocket Testament League when she was 12 years old, inviting her friends in school to read the Bible and meet Jesus.[3] As she became older and married Charles, the two of them formalized the organization, encouraging hundreds of thousands of people to adopt a lifestyle of Personal Work.

Much of their life's work was in Gospel Crusades. Charles traveled around the world four times between 1902 and 1913.[4] They both were part of huge campaigns that, in total, reached millions of people. They witnessed many people make professions of faith. Each of these campaigns included parallel efforts where Personal Work was carried out by hundreds and hundreds of people. In effect, Charles and Helen developed firsthand knowledge of the effectiveness of Personal Work as compared to large-scale evangelism. I know they would want to practice both so as to deploy many techniques to win people to Christ. Yet, like Billy Graham, with all that electrifying experience, they, and others, concluded that Personal Work was the most effective.[5]

I add to Graham's and Alexander's experience my own since leaving the pulpit. In this current season of my life, I have met more people who do this Personal Work than I have ever met before. Most don't consider themselves evangelists. They consider Billy Graham an evangelist. They consider themselves followers of Jesus.

Yet when I look at the definition of evangelism offered at the beginning of this chapter, "zealous advocacy for a cause," they certainly are evangelists. They desire not a title. Rather, they love God, they love people, and they love to connect God to people. Their labors bring real results. The results, the testimonies, pour into The Pocket Testament League, week after week, and reinforce this view of the effectiveness of Personal Work.

As I said earlier, being in the pulpit, leading Bible Studies, being part of large-scale missions, and more led me to have one perspective on evangelism. When I first came into contact with the idea of Personal Work, I certainly added this method to the vast ways we can reach others for Christ. Now, as I see the results, I am more and more convinced and—like Graham, the Alexanders, and others—it to be the most effective form of evangelism.

In chapter one, I presented my belief that if we are followers of Jesus, then we must "go & make." We are not given the option of picking and choosing which of Jesus' commands we are to follow. I find the method of Personal Work outlined in chapters three and four to be one of the *simplest* ways to obey Jesus. One of the simplest ways for me, who does not feel himself to be an evangelist.

You and I don't need another sermon about evangelism. We are not alone. Helen described how her husband considered the situation. "He always felt too much effort was made in the usual work of the churches to produce upon people a deep and powerful impression, without giving sufficient opportunity for expression."[6]

"A sufficient opportunity for expression," I love this turn of a phrase. You and I need a "sufficient opportunity for the expression" of our obedience to Jesus, our obedience to "go & make." Jesus has invited us to follow him, to love him. How can I express, to others and to God, that I love Him, that I love Jesus? Jesus told us in John 14:15-17, "If you love me, keep my commandments..." I need not another sermon. Rather, I need a "sufficient opportunity," I need to "do something" to express my love for Jesus to him.

As adults, we learn best by doing. If we want to learn how to obey, then we must put our obedience into action. We can read all sorts of books on evangelism. We can listen to sermons; even take notes! We can attend seminars and conferences and more. Yet as an adult, knowledge takes hold of us when we put it into action.

Increasing obedience and knowledge is not the endpoint. Doing Personal Work is not about mastering Scripture or checking off obedience to one more command in some long list of requirements from God. God does not work that way. Earlier it was established that God is interested in us becoming more and more like him. We know he desires none to perish (2 Peter 3:9). His heart beats for all his children. As we obey, as we do Personal Work, he grows us, and our hearts beat more and more like his.

Certainly, God could look at how we use our talents, spend our time, and even spend our money, and he would see if we were trying to be obedient (as if he doesn't already know). However, I believe what excites God more is our hearts beating in rhythm with his.

We should not be surprised at what ultimately happens next. God knows that when we fulfill what we need to do as his sons and daughters, we reap benefits. Now, most of us as Christians are taught that we obey God because we love him and not because we want to "get benefits and blessings" from him. And that is true. We should not be singularly motivated for the benefits; that would be tantamount to us trying to manipulate God. However, we will reap benefits. I want to highlight them here because Personal Work will lead you to be a person of depth and joy.

The Benefit of Personal Work

Putting our faith into action, which God knows is best for us, yields many benefits and will take us deep to the Father's heart.

The first benefit is obvious. Personal Work positively affects our outward conduct. In our workplace, in our family, in our church, everywhere. The reality that we might speak a word about Jesus has a seasoning effect on our behavior. After all, we will be presenting ourselves as Jesus' representatives and will want to present him in the best light.

of Barron's thighs. Tattoos everywhere. He felt a nudge from God to offer this man a Gospel. Then the argument started. The argument in Barron's mind. He thought no. He thought maybe it really wasn't God. Maybe it was lunch, you know, food poisoning! The arguments flowed as fast as the fuel going into the tank.

Finally, Barron succumbed to the leading. He finished pumping his gas. Made sure his credit card cleared. He went and started his car (for a fast getaway). Then, barely making eye contact with this complete stranger, a man who now seemed eight feet tall, he reached across the gas pump and gave him a Gospel of John with words to the effect that he wanted to give him a gift from God. Not waiting for a response, Barron turned, quickly got in his car, and drove away. Yay! He had done it, and he was still alive.

As he was driving and congratulating himself, he noticed in his rearview mirror lights coming up after him. He again gulped. It was the ginormous man in the mud-covered truck. Barron was approaching an intersection, and the light was turning red. He had no choice; there was too much traffic and he had to stop.

The man pulled up next to him and motioned for him to roll down his window. Reluctantly Barron complied. There, in his window, was this big burly man's man, with tears running down his cheeks. He said, "Man, God's been chasing me for three years, and I haven't known how to get back to Him. Now I do. Thank you." The light turned green and off he went. True Story. Barron was forever changed. He trusted God when he was well outside his comfort zone. God had led Barron to this man whose heart was open to receive the Living Word of God.

There are thousands of these stories through the ages. You can find many of them at The Pocket Testament League website: www.ptl.org.

The stories tell how people who never thought of themselves as evangelists answered the imperative call from God to

I ask the waitstaff their name, tell them I would love to pray for them and ask them what they might like prayer for. (The explanation to the waitstaff has a bit more to it, but I hope you get the idea).

This time I had the exact same waitress. On my previous visit, I had prayed for her and left an appropriate tip and a pocket-sized Gospel of John. I asked her if she recognized me, to which she said, "Oh yeah, I remember you." Hearing her tone caused me to gulp. But then the Holy Spirit reminded me of what I had prayed for. I responded, "I remember too, and I prayed for your fiancée; he had just left for basic training for the Marine Corps. How is he?"

The look on her face completely changed. She told me much of her story. She then asked me, "Do you remember that little book you gave me?" This time it was my turn to reply, "I remember." To which she said, "It has been on my nightstand ever since; tonight, I think I will read it!"

My heart leapt. Might that be the night, the night she opened her heart to Jesus! What a joy that moment was. What a gift from God. He did not have to arrange those two meetings. But He did! God let me see the impact His love can have on another human being.

I love Personal Work. I love Personal Work because I get out of the way and let God meet people where they, the people, are at.

I have another favorite story. It comes from a person, Barron. When he tells it, it is like a 20-minute standup comedy routine. Pure Joy! It starts with him being restless. He wanted to share his faith but couldn't figure out how. He got some pocket-size Gospels of John and put them in the glovebox of his car. They sat there staring back at him.

One night, when he was in an unfamiliar, you might say sketchy part of town, he pulled into a gas station to fill up. Soon after, a large truck, with big tires and covered in mud, pulled in right next to him. The fella who got out was huge. Biceps the size out of touch with the outside world. We become like monks and nuns without ever entering a monastery or convent. Personal Work keeps us connected to the world. The world God is reconciling to himself in Christ (2 Corinthians. 5:19).

We should not be surprised by this effect. Our Master was out among the people.

This leads to a third positive effect. We start loving people more. You might naturally ask, "How do you start loving people more?" Great question. Rather than give you theory, I highlight below just a few stories of people who opened up to me, and I was humbled. The challenges they face in life, the hurdles they overcome on a daily basis, and more lead me to pray for them. What is equally remarkable is how God, even today as I think of them, has birthed in me a real love of them.

Bottom Line: Personal Work changes my disposition for the better. Consider that I am naturally goal-oriented. I like to see things get done. I like to feel a sense of accomplishment. However, that goal orientation has an unintended consequence. I risk not seeing the people right in front of me. Personal Work changes that inside of me. It doesn't lessen my goal-driven orientation. It simply makes me more aware of the humans around me. It leads to softer language. It leads to more prayer. It leads to God's grace working through me.

I am far from a saint, and on many days, I am "not the best version of myself." But Personal Work is one practical exercise that gets me turned the right-way-round.

Finally, as we obey God, engaging people to meet Jesus, we have remarkable experiences. They can only be explained as God literally showing up—it is pure Joy!

The Joy of Personal Work

I was having dinner at a restaurant where just three months earlier, I had eaten. I travel quite a bit for my work. When I dine out,

Take one example: swearing. I used to swear like a sailor. When I became a Christian, God, in his mercy, removed this terrible habit. That was long before I began Personal Work. Yet, I cannot imagine speaking about Jesus with every other word being a "blip." I don't walk around thinking, "I better not swear." No, instead, my mind is captivated by the things of God. The more we do Personal Work, the more we will live as Colossians 3:2 encourages us to live, to have our mind set on things above.

Personal Work is a bit like exercising. You benefit from being in shape, having a good heart, and more. If you have ever had a season in your life when your diet is healthy and you sense you are getting the right amount of exercise, then you know how good you feel. The more Personal Work you do, the more you are prone to stay in spiritual shape. It is not automatic. Satan certainly would like to cause you to fall. The news is littered with Christians who have succumbed to moral failures. The alternative, however, is not to sit on the sidelines, for there, too, Satan has won.

Here is another benefit. It is internal. It is our individual walk with the Lord. Consider if we were to awake each day, and as we read our Bible and prayed, we added to our petitions of the Lord prayers for those we have spoken with in the last week.

Our prayers for them are not only for their conversion but also for the real-life concerns they shared with us. As our day goes on, we begin to see other people, asking the Lord for an opportunity to speak to them (I will get to the speaking bit in chapters three and four). Imagine if our minds are filled with these thoughts about others rather than ourselves. I have found such thoughts and prayers about others to have a positive effect on my walk with the Lord.

Such a disposition turns our focus from ourselves to others, which leads to another benefit. We become more at ease around those who do not share our faith. How easy it is, as followers of Jesus, to hang around with others who look and think exactly as we do. A natural, unintended wall forms around us. We become "go & make" – and when they "go," they do so, leaving room for God to speak to the person.

Leaving room for God allows Him to show up and share the joy. Let me explain. The natural tendency for us, as humans, is once we make up our mind to do something, we think we have to do it all by ourselves. We don't mean to, but this behavior to be independent squeezes God out of the picture.

Let me ask you. As you have been reading about "going & making," about being an evangelist, have you felt as if all the weight of this task was on you? Have you been thinking about how you couldn't do it? How you don't have the gift? It is a natural reaction.

Let me ask you another question. Did you think at all about where God fit into this new task of yours? Maybe you did. Most people don't.

I find that as people of God, when we seek to obey him, we immediately take all of the responsibility and pressure upon ourselves. I am not sure exactly why we take it upon ourselves. Humans have this tendency to think we can do everything by ourselves. To think we need help and then to ask for help is viewed by some as a weakness.

To illustrate this point, as you have been reading about Personal Work, have you been thinking that you would need to have answers to all the really hard questions. Questions like, "What about the person who lived on an island in the middle of the Pacific, who never heard the name of Jesus, did God send them to hell?" or "Why is there evil in the world?" or something even more personal "If God is a God of love, then why did he let my son or daughter die, even after I prayed to him?"

Those questions are real questions. The more sincere a person is with us, the more personal the questions become. When you take on the responsibility of sharing your faith, it is logical to think you must have the answers to these and a myriad of other questions.

Having those answers is a good thing. However, I want to make two points.

First, to try and answer those questions might be a mistake. When Jesus was asked questions, he often answered with a question. For the person who lost a child, having the perfect answer to their question of "why" will not lessen their pain. Perhaps the proper response is sorrow for their loss and prayer.

Second, the point of this book is that you do not have to be that person who can answer the very difficult questions. We call them apologists. I love folks with that gift. However, remember that sharing the Good News comes in many forms. One of those forms is simply letting God speak.

I pray you can see that doing Personal Work is effective, is beneficial, and brings Joy! It is important we don't push God out of the process, that we don't take more responsibility than God has asked. When we invite God into the process of our Personal Work, we find ourselves loving the people we engage with. We find God showing up and speaking to the very hearts of the people we engaged. All of the above brings us joy!

---

[1] Definition from Oxford Languages and Google, languages.oup.com/google-dictionary-en/, accessed May 1, 2022.

[2] Michael Green, *One to One: How to share your faith with a friend* (Moorings Publisher. Nashville, TN. 1995), p. 11.

[3] Simon Fox, *Helen Cadbury & Charles M. Alexander: A Love that Embraced the World* (Marshall Pickering, London. 1989), pp. 6–9.

[4] Cadbury, p. 183.

[5] George T.B. Davis, *The Pocket Testament League Around the World.* (The Pocket Testament League, 1910), p. Foreword.

[6] Cadbury, p. 72.

3

GOD AT THE CENTER

sov·er·eign·ty[1]
/ˈsäv(ə)rən(t)ē/

noun

1. supreme power or authority.
   "how can we hope to wrest sovereignty away from the oligarchy and back to the people?"

I have been promising in chapters three and four that I had some great news for you regards evangelism. It is twofold. First, God is in complete control—of *everything*.

> For by him all things were created in the heavens and on the earth, visible things and invisible things, whether thrones or dominions or principalities or powers. All things have been created through him and for him. He is before all things, and in him all things are held together. (Colossians 1:16-17)

The above Scripture says that not only were all things created by God but that "all things are held together." God sustains our world. The word "all" proclaims nothing is beyond God. We often use the word "sovereign" as a label for the above idea about God. Nothing surprises Him. We've already noted he does not need us to do this work.

This concept of engaging in Personal Work lines up completely with this idea of leaving room for God. We, in fact, invite God to be involved in our efforts through prayer. In the next chapter, we will spend more time on prayer; for now, let's zero in on the best tool that we can use to do the heavy lifting of a human heart. That tool is God's Voice, his very Word.

God's Voice in Our Skeptical World

At this point you might be thinking, "The Bible, really David, the Bible, that is your gift, your secret weapon?" I get your reaction. You are probably imagining me handing people a big thick Bible or hitting them over the head with verses. Let me ask you to hang in there with me because if God's Word can do this heavy lifting, would you not like to know how?

Trust me, I understand the skepticism. When I speak about God and His Word, I receive a range of reactions. Reactions from people who don't know Jesus and are angry with all that is wrong in the world and the Church, to people who do know Jesus, yet sigh and roll their eyes because they have been worn down by others who follow the Bible in an extremely aggressive manner.

Those reactions, if not thought about in love, would silence my voice. If I am honest, I myself have had those reactions to this idea of how to use God's Word. Anyone who has sought to follow Jesus has had moments of doubt and discouragement regards the Bible and its promises. For example, moments when we prayed, and his answer was no, or not yet. At those moments, we had a choice. Either conclude God was not real or is not a God of love; or conclude He loves us, has our best interest at heart, and in fact, knows more than we do about our needs in the situation.

Why might we ever conclude God loves us and has our best interest in his heart and mind? Answer: the person of Jesus Christ. Is not John 3:16 a treasured verse because it proclaims,

> For God so loved the world, that he gave his one and only Son, that whoever believes in him should not perish but have eternal life.

Many more verses, many more situations in the life of Jesus, could be cited, but the Cross proclaims not merely God's love, but the extreme depth of his love for us. As we read "God so loved the world," we read "God so loves me, and so loves you." As we read "gave his one and only son," we read "gave his one and only son to die on the Cross for me, for you." The depth of God's love is infinite.

It takes time for God's love for us to break into the deeper recesses of our hearts. However, at some point, when we conclude he has our best interest at heart, we will want to tell others about this amazing God. Yet as we seek to "go & make," as we seek to tell the world about Jesus, we are back to the "how should we do this" question.

My answer is let God speak – for himself. Think about something for a moment. If our God is actually the way he says he is, the way the Bible describes him, if he is sovereign, omnipotent, omniscient, and more, then do you think his Word cannot represent him?

Let me expand on the phrase "Let God Speak." Might we "Let God's voice be heard more than ours." Rather than our first act of evangelism being our offering to another person our ideas about God, we simply offer someone an accessible portion of God's Word.

If you think God's voice, God's Word, is a voice talking to an empty theater, then I have good news for you. People are desperate for the Word of God. There is Bible poverty in the world. How do I know people desire to receive God's Word? Because as I personally hand a small 64-page Gospel of John to hundreds and hundreds of people around the world, I watch their immediate reaction. Many of them kiss it, others cry, and still others immediately sit down and begin to read it. They treasure receiving God's Word.

And it works! Every day at The Pocket Testament League, we receive stories of people meeting God simply and powerfully through His Word, His Voice. It is a great way for those of us not necessarily gifted in other forms of evangelism to "go & make." It is a great way for us to do Personal Work.

Before I press into this idea of God's Voice, I do want to esteem the other ways that people share that God is real; share that this very real God loves them. I value all these different ways, and here a just a few examples.

Consider preaching. God's Word esteems it. Romans 10:14 clearly describes how people won't hear unless others go and tell. Preachers labor to proclaim the Good News, seeking the Lord's anointing every step of the way. Jesus himself preached. He went about proclaiming the Kingdom of God and calling all to repentance.

Consider also what the Bible calls signs and wonders: miracles. The Book of Acts over and over shows how the Apostles often first did signs and wonders. After they had people's attention, the Good News was not only proclaimed but received. Jesus used this method. He was, however, not fooled. In John chapter six, many came for earthly bread but would not receive Him who is the Bread of Life.

Consider works of mercy where God's people go and meet needs in the world. The Red Cross' symbol is not a cross by accident. The world, apart from God, is a cold and brutal place. People don't expect mercy. When it is offered, often their reaction is, "Why are you doing this?" This reaction then opens the door to sharing the love of God in Christ. Jesus' works of mercy were all born out of love, and his ultimate desire was that all would be with him forever.

Consider also those who engage the culture and expose ideas contrary to Jesus and his teaching. If Jesus and his teaching are the truth, then those opposed to him and his teaching are often promoting untruth. Untruths and falsehoods lead to death.

We are in a battle for our culture, and we need brilliant, articulate, and creative people to be apologists for the Gospel of Jesus Christ. The arguments against God are rampant. Fields of study such as science, psychology, and more have been captured by those with an agenda to eliminate God. The arts, once filled with images and stories of God, first turned away from glorifying God to glorifying man, in many ways making humankind an idol. Now art is descending from idolatry to depravity and death. Apologists in all forms are needed.

People have found more ways, very creative ways, to share the Good News, to make God's Voice be heard.

However, the purpose of this book is to encourage you to "go & make" using the very powerful voice of God. I am not interested in denigrating those other ways of evangelism. I love them. I simply want to elevate into today's discussion of evangelism the very Word of God – The Bible. The Bible is God's Word written. It is God's voice recorded with pen and paper.

Let's just dwell on that statement.

> The Bible is God's voice
> recorded with pen and paper.

If someone asked you, "Would you like to hear God's Voice today?" Not another person's explanation of what God is saying, but rather the unfiltered voice of God?" Wouldn't you say yes!

That is what is on offer to us every day. You and I can come face-to-face with the Living God and His Living Word.

I recently heard someone say, "<u>We</u> are God's <u>only</u> voice today." While I knew them and understood and appreciated where their point of view was coming from, that we need to be proclaiming the Good News in word and deed, I wanted to shout, "NO!" God's Word still speaks.

I also hear the following quote, "In all things preach the Gospel, as a last resort, use words."[2] People attribute the quote to St. Francis or St. Augustine. I cannot find anywhere where those men of God said such a thing. I understand the sentiment. And I love Matthew 5:16, which says, "Even so, let your light shine before men, that they may see your good works and glorify your Father who is in heaven."

Yet the quote, "...as a last resort use words," implies something more than Matthew 5:16. As you reflect on this quote, what do you think it implies? Some think it simply means that actions should speak louder than words. At the other end of the spectrum, I have heard preachers declare that the Bible is not to be trusted and we should let our human actions speak for God. Yet probably the most common consequence of this quote is to let Jesus' followers "off the proverbial hook." It gives us permission not to speak and not to allow God's Word to speak.

In many ways, I feel like we, Christians, are often with the best intentions, silencing God. We all, each of us, could list times when well-meaning Christians, using the Bible, said the wrong thing to another person. We could list the times we used an unhelpful Bible quote. At times, we find ourselves wincing at their words, and ours. A consequence of this, and other experiences, is that we play it safe. We do not want to offend, and we sometimes don't lead with the Word of God. Our best intentions to not offend essentially prevent God's voice from reaching people's ears (and hearts).

We need to let God's Voice be free.

> "For my thoughts are not your thoughts,
>   and your ways are not my ways," says Yahweh.
> "For as the heavens are higher than the earth,
>   so are my ways higher than your ways,
>   and my thoughts than your thoughts.
> For as the rain comes down and the snow from the sky,
>   and doesn't return there, but waters the earth,
>   and makes it grow and bud,
>   and gives seed to the sower and bread to the eater;
> so is my word that goes out of my mouth:
>   it will not return to me void,
>   but it will accomplish that which I please,
>   and it will prosper in the thing I sent it to do."
> (Isaiah 55:8-11)

We can have the best of motivations to represent God, but as verse 9 points out, our thoughts are not his thoughts. God does not need us to re-word His Living Word. In fact, it enters the world like snow and rain.

Sometimes rain and snow fall gently. Sometimes they come with a storm. God's Word is like that. God will know if He needs to blow with a gale force into our lives, or gently.

Please know, as stated earlier, I value preaching, signs and wonders, works of mercy, and more. I pray those gifted in such areas will increase their efforts. I simply want to elevate back into the fray the very Word of God. Before I share exactly "how" we elevate God's Word back into the conversation, let me share why I feel so strongly about the efficacy of God's Word. Let's go to the source.

God's Powerful Voice Is a Small Seed

I find the Parable of the Sower one of the most comprehensive teachings that:

- communicates the power of God's Word,
- the reality of the varied states of the human heart,
- and the pathway for Jesus' followers to take as they seek to "go & make."

Do you know it is found in Matthew, Mark, and Luke? (Matthew 13:1-23, Mark 4:1-20, and Luke 8:4-15) In this story, Jesus likens the way His Message, indeed the very Kingdom of God spreads, to a farmer sowing seed.

How powerful is God's Word? As powerful as a seed. A seed is small. It can be crushed. It can be eaten by birds. Yet when it is buried, when it is treated like something dead, its potential to release its power begins.

In a moment, we will dive into the different ground conditions the seed in this story encounters. For now, I want to point out that regardless of the soil:

The seed always grows.

That statement, that in the parable, except for the seed that is eaten, the seed always grows, communicates the latent potential in the seed. It is tremendous. The seed, the very Word of God, can return 30x, 60x, or 100x. This means the seed, the Word of God, planted in the heart of a person has huge potential to not only transform one life, but many!

Yet the Word of God, like a seed, can be dismissed, just as other small things in our world are dismissed. People say, "Isn't it just a book written by a bunch of men?" This is often the reaction when people either cannot understand or find a portion of it especially challenging. They want to dismiss it. Thomas Jefferson is reported to have cut out the portions of the Bible he disagreed with.[3] A sort of cafeteria plan to the Bible; pick and choose what you like, leave behind what you do not.

The Word of God, like a seed, can also be crushed. World leaders, throughout history, have banned it and burned it. Today, Voice of the Martyrs reports that in 52 countries, the Bible is either dangerous to obtain, highly restricted, or completely illegal.[4]

It is not just despots outside the church. Church leaders have told those under their charge not to read it.[5] They, the church leaders, would interpret it for them. It can be used to crush the very people it came to free. The Word of God has been used to replace the Gospel of freedom from sin, to instead enslave people to legalistic rules and traditions. And, in one of the worst chapters in the Bible's history, actually used to justify the physical enslavement of humans.[6]

Today, some of the most damaging treatment of the Scripture has been by theologians. Like modern geneticists who modify seeds to produce a different plant, these theologians have morphed the meaning of plainly written words. They have twisted and contorted the Word to, at times, mean the exact opposite.[7]

Why? Why go to all this trouble for something Jesus describes as a small little seed? Because the Word of God has power. Something that is powerless is ignored. Something that is powerful is a threat.

It has the power of life within it: new life. Those who oppose the Gospel say it is weak. Yet their actions betray their rhetoric. They openly seek to discredit it. They mock it. They work at modifying it. When they have the power, they even try to crush and ban it or twist it for their own ends. Why?

The answer is as old as Adam and Eve and the Snake. In Genesis 3:1, the serpent asked, "Has God really said...?" Satan's voice from that slithering creature made his appeal to the human heart's desire for ultimate control.

Yet we are to obey, you might say "be controlled by," God's Word. Therefore, if we do not want to be controlled by God's Word, if we instead seek to gain complete control, then we must either discredit and dismiss it or twist it into conformance with our will. Even in the Church, we wrestle against God.

Ironically, those who seek ultimate control, amid their tireless efforts to silence the Scriptures, know of the power of God's Word. They cannot stop it.

Some might wonder, "I can understand how it has power for someone who believes in Jesus, but does it have power for the non-believer?" The short answer is "yes." Let's move exactly to that question as we move from theory about the Bible to practice reading and sharing it.

God's Voice Today for Those Who Have Never Read the Words of Jesus

Returning again to this parable, when you hear the title "The Parable of the Sower," what do you remember about it? Perhaps you will pause before you read on and answer that question. What do you remember about it? Most people remember the issue of soil. Is the soil rocky, or thorny, or good? They naturally ask what type of soil would best describe them. That is a very powerful question. God's Word searches a person deeply.

I have already pointed out that:

The seed always grows.

But I notice something else:

*The sower spreads seed **everywhere**.*

The seed, the very Word of God, grows when it hits the soil. In this parable, the sower is symbolic of us, of those who want to obey Jesus' command to "go & make." So we should spread it—everywhere.

Let me share one story. It came to me in the first few weeks at The Pocket Testament League. These were my early weeks after many years of being in the pulpit. When you preach, you naturally wrestle week after week to unpack the Word of God. An unintended consequence is that it never dawned on me to simply let God's own Word do the heavy lifting of a human heart. In these early weeks, our Board of Directors was praying a very specific prayer for me; that I would come to understand the power of the Word of God. I must confess, when they told me they were praying for that area of my life, I was quite frankly surprised. After all, I was a pastor, I pridefully thought. "Certainly, I know the power of God's Word." Today, I am so thankful that was their prayer because I can tell you today that back then, I did not have a clue about the power of God's Word, simply by itself.

God answered their prayers through story after story. Here is one.

The story landed in my email during the first few weeks of my being at The League. It comes from a woman who works at a college. She was walking across a college campus when she had a chance encounter with a female student.

They began chatting, and the young girl asked the woman what she liked to do outside of work. (The student did not know she was talking to a member of The Pocket Testament League). Our member told her the same thing she liked to do at work, love people and introduce them to Jesus. Our member then asked her if she ever thought about "spiritual things"?

Isn't that a great question!

Their conversation went on for a while. Our member gave her a Pocket Testament Gospel of John and invited her to church. The student read part of the Gospel. While the student was reading, our member was praying. Praying she would see the young women again, especially at church!

The young woman came to church, they sat together and began their friendship. After another week, she offered her life to Jesus and was preparing for baptism.

After a few more weeks, the young woman called her new friend, the League member. The college student's call started with her saying, "I understand if we cannot be friends anymore." Our member was confused. The student went on to tell her the day that they met, when she was walking across the campus, she was on her way to end the life of her unborn child.

Since then, the child inside her was continuing to grow. She did not know what to do. Over and over she kept saying, "You need to know, I am not that kind of girl. I can't call my mom."

Attending college was her first time away from home. She had gotten herself in a situation that resulted in pregnancy. She could not bring herself to tell her mom or dad. She did not know what to do, so she decided to do what the world suggested.

That is the day she was handed the Word of God. That was the day the seed was planted.

After reading that story, I had to repent of the attitude I had when the Board told me they were praying I would learn the power of the Word of God. I, "the pastor," pridefully thought I knew all about the power of God's Word. I did not. Now, if you preach, please remember how much I love all forms of evangelism. I highly value preaching. My point is not to denigrate preaching but to elevate the Word of God back into the evangelism discussion, and by doing so, many more can share the Good News.

That is what God was teaching me with this story that came across my desk early in my tenure at The Pocket Testament League. The sovereign God of the universe had arranged this meeting; had arranged the planting of this seed in the soil of that young girl's heart, to not only save this young woman and her unborn child but to teach me, a prideful pastor, about the Power of the Word of God.

One last story. It is about a man who is a serious Hindu and is in jail for a financial crime. His sentence: life. He is in a country where concepts such as parole do not exist. He will die in jail.

A pastor, visiting prisoners, gave him a Gospel of John. The following week, when the pastor returned, the man came to him holding up the Gospel of John, demanding to know, "Is this true?" The pastor was startled. He did not at first understand. He said, "What are you asking? Is the entire book true?" The man said, "No, I want to know if 'this' is true." The "this" was John 1:11-13:

> He came to his own, and those who were his own didn't receive him. But as many as received him, to them he gave the right to become God's children, to those who believe in his name: who were born not of blood, nor of the will of the flesh, nor of the will of man, but of God.

The pastor said, "Yes, this is true!" He prayed with the man to receive Jesus. As he told me this story, he then asked me if I understood what had happened. I told the pastor that I understood the man had received Jesus as Savior. However, the pastor knew I did not appreciate how radical a change had taken place within the heart of the man in prison.

First of all, this pastor knows that normally a long process is required for a serious Hindu to turn to Christ. This man's acceptance happened with no other human interaction—only the Word of God. He, this pastor, was himself stunned.

Second, he observed that I was not processing the phrase "a serious Hindu." He therefore asked, "David, what do you think this man, who will die in prison, thought about every day?" That is when the penny dropped for me. This man, this serious Hindu, knew he was guilty. In his world of Karma-Dharma, he was trapped. He could not escape. He would sit each day and wonder, being tormented with the question of what his next reincarnated life would be because of his sin.

Now he is free. He will die in prison, but he is free (Isaiah 61:1). I wonder about him with his Gospel of John and his freedom. I wonder if he is not sharing so that others in prison might too be free.

The Gospel changes people. It changes nations, it changes families—and closest to home, it can change you. It can take your bitter grief and fill it with hope. It can take your fear and turn it into courage. It can take your unhappiness and turn it into contentment. It can take situations that you think are beyond God and open the door for God's love to flood into a person's life.

There is something about the Gospel, a mere seed. It is easily lost, crushed, or brushed aside. But if it gets in, and goes in deep, it has the power of life. It comes alive, it sprouts, takes root, grows, and produces fruit. That fruit produces its own seeds, not only replacing itself but multiplying.

The Bible speaks of the Word of God in other ways. It speaks of the Word as a sword or a fire; it changes people-by burning away the rotten pieces and cutting away the unhealthy parts.

For evangelism, especially where we are seeking to leave room for God to work, one-to-one seed planting is one of the best methods for our Personal Work. This parable then, with its image of a seed, visually teaches how we are to behave. We are to liberally spread and share the Word of God.

Plant the seed everywhere.

You know that the only way for a seed to release its creative power is for it to be planted. It has to go into the soil. It's the same way with the Word. If you do not plant, you are guaranteed to have no growth.

However, planting does not guarantee growth. That's the point the parable of the Sower makes with the three soils that

don't produce any lasting growth. The soils are different kinds of people.

The first soil, with its hard path, prevents the Gospel from going in at all. They are people absolutely unwilling to question or doubt themselves. So, the Gospel message of sin and salvation through Christ doesn't even receive consideration.

In the second soil, the Gospel goes in, but not very deep. There is some initial positive response to the Gospel, but then it dies. These are people who say: Good, Jesus will fulfill my agenda for happiness! They have a list of things they have to have to make life worthwhile. For a time, the religious excitement carries them along. But when Jesus doesn't produce what they want, and they suffer some losses, they fall away. They did not really want a Savior. They wanted someone to bless all they desire.

In the third soil, the Gospel goes in and begins growing. However, it goes in at the same level as the other concerns of life. The parable calls those concerns thorns. Jesus identifies these thorns as the worries of world, the deceitfulness of wealth, and desires for other things. God's Word never takes priority in the person's life, so there is never fruitful growth.

The fourth soil, the good soil, the Gospel goes in, grows, and multiplies.

I earlier asked, "But does it have power for the non-believer?" Yes! We don't know the soil. You and I will never know the condition of a person's heart (1 Samuel 16:7). The only way the living power of the Word can be released is if it is first planted. It is not our job to judge the soil, the condition of the person's heart.

That is why the Sower liberally sows seed everywhere!

God's Voice Today for Those Who Follow

For those following Jesus, I pray you will take the message of the Parable of the Sower to heart. That you will spread the Seed, the Word of God, liberally. The next chapter provides a straightforward method to accomplish this way of sharing.

Be encouraged: The reality that the seed grows independent of our ability, I pray, reinforces that you are not in this alone. God is deeply involved. You do not have to have all the answers. In reality, God the Holy Spirit works in the heart of a person to bring them into the kingdom.

The Scripture in 1 Corinthians 2:9 – 16 lays out how the Holy Spirit reveals the Wisdom of God. Verse 14 specifically says the natural person, apart from the Spirit of God, cannot understand the things of God. We have seen people, as they read the Word of God, as they hear a verse, come to faith. The scales fall from their eyes in front of us. All of this is by the Holy Spirit working in and through the Word of God.

This is why I am such a proponent of evangelism that simply shares the Word of God—without argument. There are really three parts:

- We share the Word
- The Word is Powered by God
- And God the Holy Spirit moves the human heart

Two of the three steps are God's doing, not ours. We are literally in the presence of God at work!

This leads me to want to spend some time considering the power of God's voice for those who follow. Quite simply:

We need to be people in and of the Word.

We must fill our lives with the Word of God. Listening to it, reading it, thinking about it, reflecting on it, and applying it, the

Word of God, over and over to our lives. In Ephesians 1:18, we read a beautiful prayer to people who already know Jesus, that their knowledge and love will grow deeper, that the very "eyes of their hearts will be opened."

We must not treat the Word of God as some sort of magic bean. Instead, like a garden, we must plant the seed in our own lives. Watering, weeding, and caring for the soil of our hearts. By living in God's Word, we are showing our Father how deeply we love him. Additionally, those who we share God's Word with will see our authenticity. What comes out of the soil—the words that come out of our mouth, the decisions we make, the things we do—will incline people to consider that which we are offering. They will see what is described in 1 Peter 1:22b-23, "...love one another from the heart fervently, having been born again, not of corruptible seed, but of incorruptible, through the word of God, which lives and remains forever."

Now, what am I talking about? I'm talking about more than knowing the Bible. It is not just bare knowledge of the Bible. It's working the Gospel down deep into our hearts. I will share how I try to have God's Word penetrate my heart, but first, let me share one concern.

My concern is that Bible knowledge can, if we lose our aim, rather than penetrate our hearts, harden them. Let me explain. As we spend more time in God's Word, we need to keep our aim clear. Our aim is to deepen our relationship with, and love for, God. As Christians, as we spend time in the Word, we will naturally find Bible verses coming to our minds in all sorts of situations. We may even grow to where we find ourselves quoting Bible verses at the drop of a hat. We will find the Bible guiding our lives more and more. Our goal, as we deepen our relationship, our love of God, is to follow Him more closely. However, we must be careful; we can drift into wanting to "get the rule right." Making sure we know the right way is not a bad goal. Yet, it can backfire; our aim for being in God's Word can drift from being in a relationship to rule-keeping. Bible knowledge can turn into a weapon of destruction, aiming verses at ourselves or others.

Please don't misunderstand. We need to sit under the Authority of God's Word. We need it to shape us. Romans 12:1-2 clearly implores us to be in and be changed by God's Word.

Yet, I have all too often seen it wielded not as a tool of reproof as we are told to do in 2 Timothy 3:16, but as a weapon of condemnation. I myself like to know the right answer. However, knowing the right answer, knowing the Bible, for me, can have an unintended consequence. I can allow pride to creep into my heart. I can view myself as "right" and others as "wrong." I can beat myself up in an unproductive manner each time my behavior is "wrong." And the result? I can, in the end, condemn others and myself.

When used in this destructive manner, when aimed at ourselves, the result is often depressed and anxious Christians. If we aim it at other people, we appear as proud and self-righteous Christians. In either case, the Word of God is known, but rather than draw people into a deeper relationship with the Father, it functions like a cold rule book.

The Letter of James in 1:21-25 describes our aim beautifully as he describes God's Word implanted in us so that we might be "doers of the Word."

> Therefore, putting away all filthiness and overflowing of wickedness, receive with humility the implanted word, which is able to save your souls. But be doers of the word, and not only hearers, deluding your own selves. For if anyone is a hearer of the word and not a doer, he is like a man looking at his natural face in a mirror; for he sees himself, and goes away, and immediately forgets what kind of man he was. But he who looks into the perfect law of freedom and continues, not being a hearer who forgets, but a doer of the work, this man will be blessed in what he does.

I meet people who love God's Word, people who immerse themselves in it, all the while keeping the right aim. It is a joy to spend time with them. Their lives are as full of challenging situations as the next person's, but their attitude is different. I also love when these folks speak about the Bible. For example, one person I was speaking with had a very memorable way of expressing what the Bible had taught him. "The Gospel is that I am more wicked and sinful than I ever dared to admit. And in Christ, I am more loved and accepted than I ever dared to hope."

Now regarding how I try to have God's Word penetrate my heart, please understand I am a work in progress. Some days I am better at this than others. I have a routine. I read God's Word at the same time every day. I don't think there is a universal time of day that works for everyone. Rather I think consistency and discipline are important. Reading it at the same time and reading it daily is what is important. To reinforce this idea that you can read it at different times of the day, in various seasons of my life, the time of day I read was different. When I sit down to read, I pray that God's Holy Spirit will open my heart to His Word. I read the passage several times with pen in hand. I underline. I make notes. I highlight when I have a question. I try to find a phrase or a sentence or an idea that stops me and invites me to pray. Sometimes the prayer is asking God to forgive me because I can clearly see I have not been following His Word. Other times that prayer is a prayer for strength and the ability to follow. Still other times, the prayer is a prayer of praise as I am reminded of God's love for me.

I expect the method you will develop (or have developed) to read Scripture so it penetrates your heart will be different. It's clear that if you choose to sit with God's Word and seek Him to penetrate your life with it—He will!

One such person was John Owen, a Puritan giant.[8] Amid all his writings and preaching, I once heard another preacher report that John Owen had boiled the Bible down to this short phrase,

"The Scriptures teach me three things: Who I am. Who Christ is. And who I am in Christ."

When we allow it, remarkably, the seed grows not into a complex plant. No, instead, it grows into a profound, simple, and lived truth.

As Jesus's followers, as his disciples, we are to grow in his Word, we are to spread his Word, we are to be like him: People of the Word.

---

[1] Definition from Oxford Languages and Google, languages.oup.com/google-dictionary-en/, accessed May 1, 2022.

[2] Dr. Michael A. Milton, "What Does it mean to 'Use Words Only if Necessary' When Sharing the Gospel?" *Christianity Today*. www.christianity.com/wiki/church/what-does-it-mean-to-use-words-only-if-necessary-when-sharing-the-gospel.html, accessed April 21, 2022.

[3] Alyssa Roat, "What is the Jefferson Bible?" Christianity.com www.christianity.com/wiki/bible/what-is-the-jefferson-bible.html, accessed February 27, 2021.

[4] Bible: Dangerous, Illegal, Covert by Love Packages, April 20, 2019, lovepackages.org/bibles-dangerous-illegal-covert/, accessed February 27, 2021.

[5] Jude Weber, Vatican Achieves Reveal Bible Was Once a Banned Book, January 22, 1998, www.withchrist.org/archives.htm, accessed February 25, 2021.

[6] Larry R. Morrison, The Religious Defense of American Slavery before 1830, www.kingscollege.net/gbrodie/The%20religious%20justification%20of%20slavery%20before%201830.pdf, accessed March 1, 2021.

[7] Gleason Archer, *A Survey of Old Testament Introduction.* (Moody. 2007) and Michael Wilkins, *Jesus Under Fire: Modern Scholarship Reinvents Jesus* (Zondervan , 1996).

[8] Peter Toon, *God's Statesman: The Life and Work of John Owen.* (WIPF & STOCK, Eugene, OR., 2016).

4

DON'T GET AHEAD OF YOUR GUIDE

dis·ci·ple[1]
/dəˈsīpəl/

noun

1. a personal follower of Jesus during his life, especially one of the twelve Apostles.
2. a follower or student of a teacher, leader, or philosopher.

I have been promising to give you great news for Evangelism. I pray you have picked up on some of this encouragement already.

It is not all on you: God is involved.
God is sovereign: he is in control.
God's Word has power: plant it!

Following Jesus

In those above three statements, I pray you can pause and acknowledge just how much God is in the middle of drawing people to Himself. He does not ask us to lead. He asks us to be his disciples. He asks us to follow.

Let's talk about following Jesus. In the definition of a disciple above, both choices have us following a person. For me, that means trying to follow Jesus in everything I do every day. I did not always think this way. For years, following Jesus for me was more akin to not physically murdering someone, not stealing, etc. I generally thought I was doing a pretty good job. I never really thought Jesus was expecting me to closely follow him every day. It was more that Jesus had given me some advice, a few guidelines, for how I was to go about my day.

Many Christians do make the serious move from thinking Jesus has offered a few guidelines to seriously seeking to follow him moment-by-moment. Yet we must have a critical distinction in view. That challenge is realizing we are following a person and not an idea or philosophy. Let's contrast the two.

An idea is something we understand and apply. As the idea permeates us, we can, at times, mechanically follow it without thinking. Perhaps we go even further, spending energy to study the literature, increasing our learning. Perhaps it takes such a hold on us that we spend much of our lives following this idea and philosophy. Our aim is to "master" the idea. We as masters then have this idea at our disposal as we chart the course of our lives.

This is quite the opposite of what we find in Luke 6:40, where we read a disciple is never above his teacher. A disciple is always following. Certainly, we must study God's Word and increase our knowledge. Consider Romans 12:2.

> Don't be conformed to this world, but be transformed by the renewing of your mind, so that you may prove what is the good, well-pleasing, and perfect will of God.

That does sound a bit like we are to have mastery over the Scriptures, so we can "prove" the "perfect will of God." However, one verse earlier, we are told the aim of this effort—so we can present our bodies as a living sacrifice to God. To "offer ourselves as a living sacrifice" is to be a person that comes daily to God, to Jesus, to the Master, and offers oneself.

Further, notice what Jesus says to the masters of Judaism in his day (the Pharisees, Sadducees, and Scribes). They were the most knowledgeable of God's Word, and yet they could not recognize the Author. In John 5:37-42, Jesus points out that these experts, who know the Scriptures, who even search the Scriptures to find the Messiah, can't see that the Messiah is standing before them. John 5:38 explicitly states, "You don't have his living word in you."

This is one of the unintended consequences when we approach the Scriptures as something we will master—instead of inviting the Scripture to master us.

To illustrate the point is this true story. Michael Yousef, in his book *Saving Christianity*, tells the story of two men: Charles Templeton and Billy Graham. Charles was co-founder of Youth for Christ, and he had a fiery young preacher on staff, Billy Graham. Charles concluded if he was going to be in ministry, he needed a seminary education. He enrolled in Princeton in the 1940s. There, he was filled with head knowledge. There, he began to doubt the truth of the Word of God. The story goes on to share how he would write to his good friend, Billy. He would share with Billy his growing doubt about the veracity of the Bible. Charles' doubts began to creep into Billy.[2]

Michael Yousef shared how both men, who both were filled with the knowledge of the Scriptures, ultimately reacted. Billy, one evening as he walked in the forest with his Bible, tired of wrestling with this question, knelt down, put his Bible on a tree stump, and started his prayer. "Oh, God! There are many things in this book I do not understand." He continued confessing that he had no answers to many of his friend's questions. However, led by the Holy Spirit, he ended his prayer with, "Father, I will accept this as thy Word—by faith. I will allow faith to go beyond my intellectual questions and doubts, and I will believe this to be your inspired Word."[3] The rest, you might say, is history.

Charles took a different path. While he was full of knowledge in his head about the Bible, he grew to doubt not only the Bible, but Jesus. He was interviewed at the end of his life and asked what he thought about Jesus. He gave a long eloquent answer, including that Jesus was the greatest man that ever lived. Toward the end of his answer, tears flooded his eyes, and he said, "And if I may put it this way…I miss…him."[4]

The story of these two men is stunning. Both were full of questions about God and the Bible. One, full of questions, followed the man Jesus by faith. The other, I want to suggest, was following an idea. Following this idea would cause him, as he bumped into difficult questions, to refine the idea, twisting it to conform with human reason. Unlike Billy (who chose to believe in the person of Jesus and the words of Jesus), Charles, and many like him, have refined and twisted, and refined and twisted, and refined and twisted "Christianity as an idea" so many times, that Jesus is lost. And in the end, perhaps like Charles, they tragically utter that "they miss him."

That story contains many lessons. One lesson is that we do not lead. We follow. The great news is that over and over in the Scriptures, Jesus says, "Come, follow me."[5] He is constantly inviting us to follow. He welcomes us to be with him. He has vast experience with followers who get confused, have questions, and regularly make a mess of things. Nonetheless, he desires that we follow him, that we be with him. One of the ways we can be with him, and one of the ways we learn how to follow him, is by being in God's Word.

I believe you cannot claim to be a follower of Jesus without actively planting the Word of God deeply in your heart. I shared earlier how I seek to incorporate into my daily life a discipline of reading the Bible. It does not stop there. Beyond reading, I have to put the words and commands into action. How?

I have an analogy from the non-religious world. I have had sports coaches and business mentors in my life. They would ask me to follow them, not by reading a book but by doing various exercises; at times, some of them seemed crazy. They would have me role-play various scenarios that felt completely foreign to me. Even worse, sometimes those exercises seemed to be the exact opposite of what I thought should take place. Then it would happen. A real-life situation would appear in real-time. With no time to think, I would react as I had practiced. The situation would go well. Then, after the event, it would hit me. They had prepared me. Perhaps some of you will remember the famous "wax on – wax off" scene in the Karate Kid movie.[6] It is a perfect example.

Following Jesus and His Word is like that. He certainly calls us to know His Word. He certainly calls us to obedience. Yet he is in the lead, and he will lead us. He asks us to do things that will, at the time, make no sense. The more we follow and the more we obey, the more ready we will be to serve him. He will first prepare us and then lead us to places we never imagined.

Following Jesus involves many aspects. We often pick and choose which ones we want to follow. Yet, following him means we must wrestle with all his commands, including "go & make." This book has been about encouraging you to consider making Personal Work part of your life by specifically using the Word of God.

What follows next is a simple method that will allow you to be obedient. It is a repetitive "wax on – wax off" process. This method of Personal Work seeks to practice what I have been preaching: to leave room for God. Using this method will encourage you because you will see God in action.

When we see God in action through our labors, we will realize we on not all on our own. Our trust in God will increase. We will be growing more and more into His image. In the end, we will want to keep going.

The Method

As mentioned, the method about to be described is designed to leave room for God. This method has been used by The Pocket Testament League since 1893. It works. As of the year 2020, millions of followers of Jesus, disciples, have invited over 150 million people to meet Him.

Just a reminder: don't confuse *simple* with *easy*. The Method is best described as Read—Carry—Share ®.

Step One: Read.

Read God's Word every day. Earlier I shared how I seek to read God's Word. Find your way. Above all, read it *daily*!

Step Two: Carry.

When you finish reading, pray something like, "Lord, lead me to the person you want me to offer your Word to today," <u>and then</u> put a Gospel of John in your pocket or purse. This step not only prepares you to be ready with a Gospel but also invites God into the process. He will lead you to people He has prepared.

Step Three: Share.

As the Lord leads, offer a Gospel of John to a person with words of encouragement. Who knows, perhaps He will lead you to a ginormous man with a mud-covered truck at a gas station! The Appendix contains many examples regarding exactly how to share the Gospel with a person, and perhaps, right now, your mind is taking you to a specific person you desperately want to meet Jesus.

What is your reaction?

I want to share with you the comments and reactions I have received after presenting this method to thousands of people.

First, I expect you can understand why we call it Read-Carry-Share ®. Right now, I wonder if some reading about this method are thinking what I have heard from many people? Are you thinking it is too simple, too cute even? Are you thinking there is no way a person will meet Jesus and, further, be discipled? Let me ask you to pause and try and identify what you think about Read—Carry—Share ®.

If you are thinking the process is too simple, consider what God could do in this process. What if God actually led you to the person who needed an encouraging word and the Word of God. What if God's part of this was that when the person you had given the Gospel to, when they sat down and read the Word of God, the Holy Spirit was there? Do you believe those possibilities exist in God's world?

I bring up God because when I first heard of this method of evangelism, I had lots of questions. I wrongly focused on what I perceived as the minimum physical action of reaching my arm forward and offering someone a pocket-sized Gospel of John. My mind was asking, "Doesn't the person need an explanation from me?" Certainly, I should explain the Good News. Yet, that is not the process. I couldn't, in my wildest imagination, think handing someone a Gospel of John in an accessible format, without arguing, and at times without further human interaction, would yield results. I had not allowed myself to envision that God would be present. I had not considered that God might have been working in the heart of the person he was leading me to share the Gospel of John with.

The other mistake in my thinking was that I had never really done it. I had never seen the look on a person's face when this gift of God's Word was given to them. I had no legitimate data for criticism.

Further, I failed to consider a number of other aspects. I had failed to appreciate the Read and Carry (pray) steps. I had failed to appreciate how doing that every day would change me. Those aspects of diligently reading God's Word daily and praying to meet people is a discipline very much like "wax on – wax off." Doing so prepares us to actually engage people when the Lord leads us to share.

Doing this work has yielded results in me. I have a long way to go, but I have become a better follower of Jesus. A better follower not because of what I have done but because I have seen God in action! Doing this work has also led me to identify some challenges and pitfalls.

Challenges, Pitfalls, and Lies

The Challenge of Fear

The first challenge that people often experience is fear. The process, while simple, does require you to engage another human, often a stranger. This naturally leads to the question of how to offer a Gospel, which is immediately followed by the next question. How will the person we offer the Gospel to respond? What will they say? What if the person reacts angrily? What if they ask me a question and I cannot answer? The "what ifs" pile up, fear grows, we freeze, and we don't offer someone a Gospel of John.

How do we overcome this fear? We need to remember we prayed, and we are following God's leading. Further, the Appendix offers many ways and suggested words to use when offering someone a Gospel of John to read. Further, God loves it when his children are obedient. As we seek to obey, I know God is with us, especially during those early steps of obedience.

Perhaps an analogy might help. The human image I have in my head is a parent teaching their child to ride a bicycle. Many children are fearful as they stare at the bike. They wonder if they can really do it. The parent, running alongside for a distance, adds confidence. Then, at the right moment, mom or dad let go!

From the child's perspective, with mom or dad's hands on the bike, they feel secure. At the moment those parental hands release them, there can be quite a wobble in their steering. Soon, however, they pick up speed and begin steering. That doesn't mean the parents are done parenting or the child is done learning. It simply means both are growing. Learning to master riding will take time. The new rider will hit some potholes. The new rider might get caught in a downpour of rain and get soaked. The new rider, however, can also experience freedom!

Having invited people to meet Jesus with a Gospel of John for years, I can tell you that those early times of sharing is a bit like learning to ride a bike. Early on, I felt God right there, and yes, there was a little wobble in my voice. Over time, I have grown more proficient and comfortable in engaging people. Finally, I want to tell you the fear doesn't completely drain away. Every now and again, it rears its head.

Fear is Satan's weapon, and he wants you to stop inviting people to meet Jesus. I still can have a tinge of fear, especially in situations where I might feel uncomfortable. I ask myself, "Should I really do this now?" Then, I ask the Lord, "Lord do you want me to offer this person your Word?" The Lord has not let me down. I have never had a person yell at me or even be mean. I have had people decline to receive the Gospel. Most of the time, they receive it with joy. Many times, a conversation ensues. Not a heavy theological conversation, but a conversation about what is taking place in their personal lives.

I remember two encounters in particular.

The first was when I was at lunch with some other people. I asked my waiter their name and explained that while I was giving thanks to God for the food, I would love to pray for them, so I asked them, "How can I pray for you?"

The waiter was being highly professional. Doing his job and not being intrusive. When I inquired about praying for him, his face completely changed. He said, "I got very bad medical news yesterday." Imagine that moment. I simply said, "Wow, I'm sorry, and you're at work today." He replied it was good for him to be at work. So I told David (that was his name) we would pray. And we did. At the end of the meal, I left him a proper tip and a Gospel of John. We exchanged a few short words, and he thanked me. He had been carrying that frightening medical news and had not shared it with anyone. Telling it to us at our table allowed him to at least say it out loud. Yes, we were complete strangers, but God provided us to him, so he could at least say it out loud. I left him a Gospel of John that day with a supportive note. I pray it helped him have the courage he needed to tell those close to him the challenging news. I have no idea if our encounter changed him. That was in 2016. I have never seen him again, yet I still think of him. I still pray for him. Are you getting a sense of how God is working in me?

In another restaurant scene, I was with a large group of people in a major city. The city setting was leaving me feeling a bit intimidated. By now, my friends know that I ask the waitstaff how I can pray for them. They were waiting for it. I was not sure I wanted to. I knew my hesitation was fear. By God's grace, I overcame the fear, and I asked the waiter how I could pray for him. At first, the waiter did not understand what I was telling him. He did not understand the prayer thing. First, he said, sure, I could pray at the table, just quietly. He did not understand I wanted to pray for him. It took two more times. Each time my anxiety grew. He and I finally got it sorted out, and then he thought for a moment. He asked me to pray for his mother. He then went to the next person to take their order. I thought,

"Whew, I did it," but I had this little voice of doubt regarding whether or not I should have engaged this waiter. I was asking myself if God had truly led me to speak to the waiter.

After he had gotten about halfway around the table taking people's orders, he looked straight at me and walked back to me. Internally I gulped. I thought, "Here we go. I knew I shouldn't have asked." He came to me and asked in an inquiring tone, "Will you really pray for my mom?" My response was, "Absolutely. I will pray for your mom, Mary. That is my mother's name as well!" And, I added, "I will pray for you." He replied, "That is the <u>nicest</u> thing anyone has ever done for me." Then he went back to taking our orders. When our meal ended, he and I had a great conversation. I learned about his hopes and aspirations for his life. As I handed him a Gospel, I learned a little about why he was struggling with my request for prayer. Responding to what I learned about his life, I said, "I hope those dreams of yours come true. I want to give you this little book. The message inside it completely changed my life for the better." He skeptically asked, "Is this a Christian thing?" I answered, "Yeah, but don't let Christians or the Church get in your way; it is a really a Jesus thing." He smiled.

Imagine as he was taking our orders what was going through his mind. He walked back to me, asking if I was really going to pray. He had been processing this crazy question from me. His conclusion was if I really was going to pray that, "…it was the nicest thing anyone had ever done for him."

Was what God led me to do that big a deal? In one sense, we might say no. In another sense, it was and is. The waiter's name, his person, was brought into the very Throne Room of God and presented in prayer. Is that why he said it was the nicest thing? Did he get that bit? Or was it because his life had been so hard, that he had been shone so little kindness, that this small act of love shone through the darkness of his world? I don't know. I do know that the Lord humbled me that day because I almost chickened out.

This is why we must not give in to our fears. The action you can take to address any fear is to lean into God's Word. Commit your daily "Read" step to this for a month. Consider simply doing a study where you look at what the Bible says about fear. Here is a start: consider owning these three bits of Scripture:

- Psalm 27:1
- Deuteronomy 31:6
- Psalm 118:6-7

The Pitfall of Familiarity

Beyond fear, there is a pitfall—familiarity. As humans, as we gain experience and proficiency with sharing a Gospel of John, we can inadvertently skip the "Read" and/or "Carry" step. Suddenly, we are out in public, handing out Gospels, having not invited God into the process.

In order to try to keep myself from this error, I tend to use a bit of sarcasm with myself. I tell myself:

Don't treat God like a gumball machine.

Do you remember gumball machines? How about those prize machines with the claws? They are the bane of a parent's life when they take their children to the grocery store. Lined up at the entrance/exit are these shiny machines, some with flashing lights. They are just the right height for kids. Simply put in some money, work the machine, and out comes your surprise: a gumball or a toy. It works 100% of the time. Money in—prize out!

This method of Read—Carry—Share ® is not you or I having God at our disposal. It is not that we hand a Gospel out and a person accepts Jesus. While the discipline of daily reading God's Word and daily asking Him to lead us may seem formulaic, it is not meant to be that way. It is meant to place ourselves before God, to seek his involvement, and to follow. We are like the

sower, spreading seed as the Lord leads, all the while not knowing the condition of the human heart.

Remember the bike analogy? I mentioned that a rider may get caught in a downpour. Nowadays, I can tell you when I get caught in a downpour, I have skipped step one and/or two. I do not mean to skip those steps, but the busyness of life can get the better of me. Yet the result is I am foolishly behaving as if I am doing this work of invitation all in my own strength.

When we seek his leading, we are literally engaging with God. We are journeying with him. We are putting ourselves at God's disposal, not the other way around. We will then come in contact with the people he has chosen. When we pause and ask, "Lord is this the person I should share your Word with?" We put ourselves into God's service, AND we actually begin to see the other human as a person. When I asked my typical question, I've literally had one waitstaff sit down at the table and begin crying. I was with a coworker, and the time we spent together, as complete strangers, was exactly what God provided for his child in need. That God would actually use us in this way to reach others is humbling.

To avoid falling victim to this issue of familiarity be disciplined about Reading and Carrying. These first two steps will ground you, with God always in the lead.

The Challenge to Silence the Lies

The third challenge is that of our minds. The Father of Lies will not be happy with you. He will fill your head with all sorts of lies. They are meant to prevent you from reaching out.

- He will tell you people won't like you.
- He will tell you people will think you are one of those Christian weirdos.

- He will tell you that your friends won't want to be with you.
- He will tell you the specific person you are thinking of engaging will lash out at you.
- He will tell you the waiter will probably spit in your food (yes, this is what he tells me).
- He will tell you that a little Gospel of John won't work.
- He will tell you the person won't read it.
- He will tell you that person might not be able to read.
- He will tell you that you are a sinner, a terrible sinner, that you are not holy enough to share God and God's Good News.
- His list is endless.

Why do I include such an exhaustive list? Because I want you to know Satan is relentless with his lies. Rebuke the lies.

You and I are not the first to face this situation. God's Word has two letters the Apostle Paul penned to a church he cared deeply about. While Paul's name is so often attached to these letters, I remind myself it is God's voice

> But I am afraid that somehow, as the serpent deceived Eve in his craftiness, so your minds might be corrupted from the simplicity that is in Christ.
> (2 Corinthians. 11:3)

Notice two items. First, Satan has been using this tactic for a long time. Second, notice where the attack is aimed – our minds. So we must prepare our minds. This situation reinforces an earlier point from Charles Alexander.

> The last thing the devil will let you do is win a soul definitely to Christ. If you don't believe it, try it. He will let you never miss a prayer meeting or Sunday service; he will even let you get up and lecture on religious subjects and do all sorts of religious deeds if you will stop short of one thing—get face-to-face with individuals, to bring them to a decision for Jesus Christ, and to get them to confess Him openly before the world.[7]

Why? Because Satan knows that the Word of God, offered in love by one saved sinner to another, has the power to break through his lies and draw a person to God. Satan can see in the spiritual realm what you and I cannot see. He can see the battle being fought to save that soul. And he knows who wins. This work, this Personal Work, is terribly important.

At this point, as I have done with the earlier two challenges, I would suggest some actions you might take. Rather than list a short set of actions, I want to dig into why our daily health of following Jesus, you might say our holiness of life, is critical.

The Need for the Holiness of Our Lives

As we go about this work, especially in light of the comment I just made regards how terribly important this Personal Work is, I want to return to a point made much earlier.

God does not need us to do His work of redeeming His good creation. He lets us. He, in fact, uses this work as much to build us up as his followers as to reach those who have yet to hear his name.

This point of "building us up" brings me back to an earlier point in chapter two regarding how we need to do this work as much for ourselves as for those who have yet to meet Jesus.

It makes me think of how economies work. In God's economy, there is no waste. He takes the effort we offer for evangelism and uses it to make us more and more his disciples.

As you and I are daily in God's Word and daily praying to the Lord, He works in us. Simply look again at the Parable of the Sower.

Just like a seed that takes root and grows and starts to produce things, the seed planted in us does not stay small. It produces new life--in us.

I never thought of myself as an evangelist. I still don't. I think of the giants such as D.L. Moody and Billy Graham as people to whom that title applies. Yet I will tell you that I now see ways, new ways, that God is working in and through me that I did not see before. New attitudes. New abilities. A tremendously expanded life. I see people more than I did. As a goal-oriented person, I am so often singularly focused on my world. So much so as to ignore others. Now, as I pray, "Lord, lead me to the person you want me to share this Gospel with," in his mercy, he allows me to see other people and their worlds.

Jesus says in John 10:10b, "I came that they may have life, and may have it abundantly." The grammar in the Greek reveals that this statement from Jesus means he wants to give us life, an abundant life, now! Abundant life means we can see things we never saw before.

- The love of God the Father.
- The reality of heaven and hell.
- Our own sinfulness and need for repentance.
- Our infinite personal value in the eyes of God.
- The righteousness of Christ—and Christ in us.
- The hope of the resurrection.

We know that the existence of God is not hidden; everyone can see Him, for we read in Romans 1:19-20:

> ...because that which is known of God is revealed in them, for God revealed it to them. For the invisible things of him since the creation of the world are clearly seen, being perceived through the things that are made, even his everlasting power and divinity, that they may be without excuse.

But when the Word of God comes into our life, we start to see things differently. Now at this point, you might be asking, "What does any of this have to do with evangelism and with the holiness of life?"

I want to suggest that coming to faith in Jesus as God come to earth, faith that we need Him as our savior, and by faith, receiving Him as our savior, is just the beginning of our walk. Just as when we first came to faith, God revealed spiritual realities to us, so too, when we put our faith into practice, He will reveal new realities of both himself and this world.

Unfortunately, many of us stop short of living out our faith. When we stop short of living our faith, we stop growing and shunt the life that God has planned for us. God intends for us to grow. We are meant to live the fullest lives for Christ.

This brings me back again to a point in chapter two regards the benefits of Personal Work. It has an immediate impact on our lives. As we offer people Jesus, we are reminded by God the Holy Spirit to pay attention to our own spiritual condition. Let me use some extreme examples. I doubt we would be at a bar, inebriated and sharing a Gospel of John, or a brothel or a casino. As Charles Alexander would say, "Personal Work causes you to live a clean life."[8]

Yet "living a clean life," as Charles points out, does not happen effortlessly. In fact, Satan will stir up all sorts of temptations in an effort to stop you from sharing. Imagine if we are caught up in some sin, and we then go to share a Gospel. The Enemy's voice will be very loud in our minds, seeking to discourage us.

None of us, as we seek to follow Jesus, have arrived at our destination perfect in Christ. We are works in progress. We are "under construction." All of us have areas of our lives that are not in alignment with God's will. For some of us, it may be one or two areas that we just cannot seem to get right. We label those as "besetting sins." Hebrews 12:1 actually gives us the solution for those "sins which so easily entangle us/cling to us." The solution is "run the race." Don't focus on the sin; focus on living a life devoted to God.

In religious lingo, we talk about this dimension of our life as our holiness. It can be an uncomfortable word. We don't want to behave as "holier than others." Yet I want to encourage us to focus on being holy. God tells us in Leviticus 19:2 and 1 Peter 1:16, "to be holy for I am holy."

Quite simply, God wants 100% of each of us. He wants all of us to be strong in him for our benefit. I have found Personal Work to be a wonderful, daily reminder of my need to keep, as it says in Hebrews 12:1, running the race.

Personal Work benefits us but is not for our benefit alone. It benefits those who receive our kind words with a small, powerful gift. Personal Work, through God, brings results.

Results

I am not sure it is possible for me to imagine the scene in heaven described in Revelation 7:9, "...I looked, and behold, a great multitude, which no man could count, out of every nation and of all tribes, peoples, and languages, standing before the throne and before the Lamb..." I know that at a cosmic level, some of those gathered, I believe millions, are from this simple Read—Carry—Share ® method.

This Pocket Testament League method is a seed sowing method. When you think about how a seed produces fruit, you realize it, in turn, produces its own seed, which leads to more fruit, that, in turn, produces seed. You get the idea.

Let me give you a specific example. The Pocket Testament League restarted its work in China in 2009. One of the people who helped us re-start already knew us. He had been reached by The Pocket Testament League in the 1940s before all missionaries were expelled.[9] He could trace his coming to Christ from the first work of The Pocket Testament League in China in 1909. He was an example of multi-generational fruit. A real example of seed-fruit-seed-fruit-seed-fruit!

For years, The Pocket Testament League has published stories of transformation and change in its Annual Report & Inspiring Stories book. It shares this book with its members, and you can read many of those stories at www.ptl.org/stories.

Results to Come

As believers, we commonly lament the state of the world. One of my responses to such sentiments is, "If you don't like the harvest, plant more seeds." I truly am not trying to sound sarcastic. I believe in this method.

I said that to someone, and they responded, "The ground is too hard to plant seed around here..." Can I just add one more bit to what I have been saying? It is about how God works in the world.

If you study all the Scriptures, you note that God uses time to allow tension to build up. At just the right time, he starts "shaking the earth." Think about how long Abraham waited for the birth of one son, 25 years from God's first promise. Think about how long the Israelites were slaves in Egypt, 400 years. God needed that length of time to build up tension. Why? So that when God begins to move, when he sends people like Moses, like Jesus, we will act!

God allows all that tension to build, not because he is mean. Rather, he knows us. He knows we need to see the world in sharp contrasts before we will take the risk and act. When enough tension has built up, he starts shaking. When he shakes, he is breaking up the hard ground. The ground that the seed, the Word of God, heretofore could not penetrate.

Consider our situation in the early part of the 21st century. First, there are more followers of Jesus than there have ever been. Second, we have within our lifetime the opportunity to translate the very Word of God into every language on the globe.[10] Third, the largest wealth transfer in the history of the world is taking place[11], and the "Christian" part of that wealth transfer has been studied. The conclusion? We have at our disposal a surplus of the financial resources needed to reach every people group in the world! This is the first time in the history of the world we have been in this position. These conditions have never before been present!

My brothers and sisters, God is shaking. He is shaking the earth. The largest migration of people in the history of the world is taking place right now.[12] In 2020, 19% of all migrants came to the United States.[13] What do we know when people migrate? They are open to listening to the Gospel.

God is shaking still. Muslims are accepting Jesus as their Lord and Savior more than ever before in the history of the world. Even the mainstream media is reporting it.[14]

In 2020 and into 2022, a global pandemic has taken hold. This is not beyond God. I sat having dinner in a country that suffers terrible religious persecution. Our conversation was about all the new challenges and restrictions a very oppressive government had recently enacted. An Elder, someone who had been imprisoned for his faith, was eating quietly and listening. Finally, he was asked his opinion. He spoke with authority. He said, "All of this is not the government. God is in control. God is disciplining us. He needs us to be stronger and tougher. Persecution will grow, and God needs us to be tougher. Everything is under God's control and by His plan." We all sat there in silence, knowing he was right. He returned to quietly eating. It was quite the "drop the mic" kind of moment.

Finally, I would add that evil is growing. The Book of Revelation tells us that as we grow closer to the end, both evil and good will grow. In other words, we will be able to see the sharp distinction between light and darkness—those gray moral areas will disappear.

My brothers and sisters, God is shaking. Hard ground, hearts hardened to God, are being broken up by Him. There is an urgency to this work. We are not to delegate it to some small group of Jesus' followers. All of us must do this Personal Work of evangelism. Fear not; God has given us the most powerful tool of all time: His very Word.

It is time to spread seed.

---

[1] Definition from Oxford Languages and Google, languages.oup.com/google-dictionary-en/, accessed May 1, 2022.

[2] Michael Yousef, *Saving Christianity*. (Tyndale Momentum. 2020), p. 10.

[3] Ibid. p. 11.

[4] Ibid. p. 13.

[5] Matthew 4:19, 9:9, 10:38. Mark 2:14, 8:34, 10:21. Luke 9:23, 18:22. John 1:43, 10:27, 12:26, 21:22.

[6] Youtube video of a portion of the movie *Karate Kid*. www.youtube.com/watch?v=SMCsXl9SGgY, accessed February 28, 2021.

[7] Cadbury, p.12.

[8] Ibid, p.12.

[9] In 1909, Charles and Helen Alexander landed in China for the first time (Cadbury, p. 163). Later, in the 1940s, The Pocket Testament League was extensively in China as chronicled in the book *Good News for China*.

[10] Greg Pruett, *Illuminations: A Bible Translation in Every Language by 2033*, christianstandard.com/2021/11/illuminations-a-bible-translation-in-every-language-by-2033/, accessed May 10, 2022.

[11] Mark Hall, The Greatest Wealth Transfer in History, www.forbes.com/sites/markhall/2019/11/11/the-greatest-wealth-transfer-in-history-whats-happening-and-what-are-the-implications/?sh=226483a94090, accessed May 10, 2022.

[12] www.un.org/en/global-issues/migration.

[13] citizenpath.com/countries-with-the-most-immigrants/.

[14] www.newsweek.com/christianity-islam-turning-jesus-1446327

5

WHY THE GOSPEL OF JOHN?

Asking a former pastor with a few seminary certificates hanging on the wall "why the Gospel of John?" runs the risk of falling into a deep well. I could write a treatise in answering this question. However, let's keep it simple. Here are five reasons.

1. The author tells us the specific reason he wrote it.

The author, St. John, in his Gospel, in 20:31, writes, "…but these are written, that you may believe that Jesus is the Christ, the Son of God, and that by believing you may have life in his name."

The first reason to use the Gospel of John is because its author tells us the specific reason he wrote it. His purpose is that people will be faced with a choice after they read it, to receive by faith the grace that Jesus is the Christ, the Son of God, and thereby have life today and life forever—or reject Him! To be clear, the Holy Spirit inspired John to write it with this purpose. No other Gospel makes this claim. This means the author intentionally sat down with the aim of reaching people who did not yet know Jesus as Savior.

2. In the first 14 verses, you will meet Jesus, you will meet yourself, and you will be given the Good News.

St. John does not mince words. He wastes no time.

You will meet Jesus

Consider how John starts:

> In the beginning was the Word, and the Word was with God, and the Word was God. The same was in the beginning with God. All things were made through him. Without him, nothing was made that has been made. In him was life, and the life was the light of men. (John 1:1-4)

John begins his Gospel with Jesus being present before the universe was created. John starts not with Jesus born of a human mother. Neither does he start with connecting Jesus with a long genealogy linking Jesus' humanity to either Adam or Abraham (as do Luke and Matthew, respectively). No, John starts with Jesus as the author of creation.

This is not a biography of Jesus but an Apology that Jesus is not only God, but he is God come to earth to save what He created by being the Christ. John specifically chose only seven signs or miracles to show Jesus' power.

- Turning water into wine at a wedding in Cana (2:1-11) reveals how Jesus has command over the created universe. Atoms change at his command!

- Healing an official's son in Capernaum (4:46-54) draws our attention that Jesus' power is not bound by space or distance.

- Healing an invalid at the Pool of Bethesda in Jerusalem (5:1-18) communicates, among other things, that time is not a factor. The man had his illness for over 38 years.

- Feeding the 5,000 near the Sea of Galilee (6:5-14) is not a magic trick. In John's Gospel, Jesus creates food literally out of nothing—just as God did in Genesis 1:1-3.

- Walking on the water of the Sea of Galilee (6:16-21) is Jesus demonstrating his power over the forces of this world.

- Healing a blind man in Jerusalem (9:1-7) brings Jesus into contact, and conflict, with the religious leaders of the day. His healing remarkably reveals that some will be blind to who he really is.

- Raising Lazarus from the dead (11:1-44) should silence all his opponents. The ultimate consequence of sin, death, is reversed at the simple command of this Man from Nazareth.

John's Gospel, with all its twists and turns, presents these seven signs which transcend the physical world and leave no doubt that Jesus is the Christ, the Son of the Living God. Jesus is God, and he has come to earth. It really cannot be much clearer.

You will meet yourself

We will read in John 1:10 that "the world did not recognize him." We don't recognize him, at least not on our own. Without the Holy Spirit leading, we will not be found by Jesus. We will be separated from God.

This separation has dire consequences as we turn to embrace a life apart from God, a life of sin. Later in John 3:19, John more explicitly makes this point, "men loved the darkness rather than the light." In that one statement is a summary of the rebellious human heart. For some, the darkness is so overwhelming they do not know him.

You will receive the Good News

In John 1:12-13, the text goes on to say,

> But as many as received him, *to them he gave the right to become God's children*, to those who believe in his name: who were born not of blood, nor of the will of the flesh, nor of the will of man, but of God. (emphasis added)

These are the exact verses that spoke to the Hindu man in jail highlighted above in chapter three.

This is the Good News. We can become members of God's family if we would only receive Jesus in our hearts.

All of this is done in 14 verses! You would think John's Gospel was written for those of us living in the "sound-bite-world" of the 21st century. Today, in our world, we are told to "get to the point!" We have the attention spans of gnats. John's Gospel is perfect: it gets right to the point.

3. It is somewhat like the Cliff Notes of the Bible.

The third reason to use the Gospel of John is because it is somewhat like the Cliff Notes of the Bible. Let me explain. If you know your Bible, then you hear the echoes of its great themes and stories running through these 21 chapters. Consider these short descriptors of some of the chapters:

- Chapter 1, verse 1: "In the beginning...." Hello, anyone hear Genesis?

- Chapter 1, verse 36: "Behold the Lamb of God." Anyone hear Passover Lamb?

- Chapter 3, verse 14: "As Moses lifted up the serpent in the wilderness." Here is the foreshadowing of the saving Cross of Jesus.

- Chapter 6, verse 31-35: "He (Moses) gave them bread to eat from heaven." Jesus declares himself the Bread of Life.

- Chapter 7, verse 37: Jesus says, "If anyone is thirsty, let him come to me and drink." In the Old Testament, Ezekiel prophesies that Living Water will flow out of the Temple. At the very festival which celebrates this Scripture, Jesus declares himself this Living Water.

The list goes on. John's Gospel is a short yet brilliant and powerful story that connects to the many touch points of the Old Testament. It does so effortlessly.

Imagine John's Gospel being a person's first encounter with the Bible. Imagine them coming to faith in Jesus. Then imagine, as they begin to read the Bible for the first time, they recall these wonderful moments when they first read the Gospel of John.

4. The Explicitness of John's Gospel

The fourth reason is the explicitness of John's Gospel. There is no beating around the bush, as it were. In John's Gospel, we will read in John 3:16, "For God so loved the world." We will hear from Jesus' own lips in John 14:6, "I am the way, the truth, and the life." And John 14:6 continues, "No one comes to the Father, except through me." I could keep on going. John, because his purpose is that people would be challenged to accept Jesus, does not mince words at critical moments. He wants to confront us with the very Person of Jesus.

This Gospel has been attacked by many New Testament scholars.[1] These same scholars deny the virgin birth, the miracles of Jesus—indeed his very resurrection. Because John's Gospel is so direct, the only way they can discredit the text is through a direct assault. This is not new. During the second half of the second century A.D., Celsus attacked Jesus' incarnation and resurrection.[2] The attacks continue. While we know that in the end, God prevails, we should not be surprised. Nor should we abandon the truth of God's Word.

5. John's Gospel speaks to the worldviews of his day *and ours*.

Our fifth reason is that John's Gospel speaks to the world views of his day and ours. Powerful philosophical forces are afoot. They are in the air we breathe. John's Gospel stands against these forces, inviting us to seriously look at them from a biblical perspective.

Rather than survey the Gospel for all the various philosophical points it challenges, let's just start with the first three words of John's Gospel: "In the beginning..."

Those three words turn secular theories on their head. Consider this question. When did people think the universe had a beginning? Always? The answer is no. You and I have grown up with the "big bang theory." We take it for granted. For centuries, since Aristotle, the prevailing view of philosophers, and later scientists, was that the universe was always here. Crazy right?

Certainly, some would argue the point, but they did not use the Bible to do so. Nor did their arguments win the day.

Returning to John's Gospel: "In the beginning..." Yes, you might hear Genesis, but to those non-Jews (which was most of the world), the universe always existed. The dominant worldview rejected the Jewish creation narrative. It rejected that the world had a beginning. All of that was sheer fantasy. Now is this a big deal? Yes.

John, as the Holy Spirit inspires him to write this masterpiece, with three words, simultaneously captures the attention of the secular and sacred world. Jews would hear Genesis. Gentiles (which is the label Jews gave everyone else in the world) would be shocked. They just assumed the universe was always present. I wonder if they yelled in confusion, *"What?"*

In the world of philosophy, to say the universe had a beginning is to immediately (and I mean immediately) force the next question: "Who?" Who caused this "thing," this beginning, to happen?

If there was a beginning, then someone or something set it in motion. And that is just too big a question because it implies something, or someone, exists "outside" of that which has been created.

Let me dig deeper. In John 1:1, we read, "In the beginning was the Word, and the Word was with God, and the Word was God." The Greek language uses the "word" *logos* which we translate as "word." So what is the big deal?

The word *logos* had a deeper meaning than letters on paper. Greeks, since the sixth century before Jesus, wrote about an idea, an idea they labeled *logos*. They defined this word as the fundamental thought, or organizing principle, or force if you will allow, that then causes the universe to not only come into being but to be held together.[3] The Greeks (like many today) marvel that any of the universe is here. And not just here, but we are here alive. And we are not just here alive, we are here alive, and we can observe how ultimately amazing all "this" is!

Picture the scene as the Greeks first read John's Gospel. "In the beginning was this idea, this ordering principle, this force. And this principle was with God." The Greeks would think, "Sure, the idea, principle, or force that caused all of this is with

God. But John presses on. John says this idea, principle, or force that you Greeks think brought everything (everything = this amazing, complex, beautiful world) into being is NOT outside of God but is God.

I expect the Greeks would get nervous. They might say, "Now when you say God, what do you mean?"

But before they can take John down that road of debate, he presses on. John then writes, "He was in the beginning with God. Did you catch it? "He," the original text is clear. John switches from an abstract idea to a PERSON. He, Jesus, was in the beginning. And he does not stop there. John 1:2 proclaims that "All things (everything) were made through him. Without him, nothing (read again, not a single atom) was made that has been made." WOW!

This view blows the minds of the Greeks, challenging their views. John's Gospel puts the intellectual elite on notice. It demands they respond. It forces them to expose their assumptions.

John simply declares that God is the prime mover. He caused it all. He owns it all. And most wildly, He who was outside the universe breaks into his world and becomes flesh and dwells among us.

It is not just the intellectual elite of John's day but the intellectual elite of our own day. Several years ago, the debate regarding the origins of our existence, between The Big Bang and Intelligent Design, raged, with book after book being published.[4]

For centuries, the scientific community was somewhat content to proclaim, "The universe always was." What a comfortable assumption. It avoids that messy question mentioned earlier. The question of "who caused it?"

In the 20th century, scientists began observing and measuring bits of the universe. They saw it expanding. Could it be that the universe had a beginning? This theory was first posited in the 1920s.[5] It was resisted. It was resisted by the likes of Einstein.[6] If there was a time when the universe "was not" to be followed by a time when it "was," then, if we are to be intellectually honest, we have to deal with that pesky question: "Who or what are those forces which caused all this?"

John says the world has a beginning and the person who caused it was God. It was Jesus.

Yet even as the Big Bang pressed into accepted science, for years after, we have lived in this world of evolutionary coincidence. It just happened that the cosmic forces brought this all about. Those opposed to God cried out, "Our existence is all just chance!"

But science, when it seeks objective truth, runs into The Truth.

Today we have had to face what people call Intelligent Design. Eric Metaxas, in his book *Miracles,* notes that when Carl Sagan proclaimed, "There is the universe, and that is all there is," he had behind him two, just two, unchanging scientific natural laws that must always be true for the earth, with the right level of oxygen (and everything else) to exist, so we could exist. People would look at the probability that these two "constants" could evolve into being. The probability wasn't bad. It was about .001, or .01%. [7]

Today, however, we know that it is not two "unchanging natural laws," but over 20. The probability is staggering. The situation is vastly beyond Sagan's past thinking.

The other issue is evolution and time. In the past, when the universe "always was," scientists would simply say, "Well, given enough time, things evolved to what we have today." But today, the world of science has now established when the universe began, and they realize there simply is not enough time for all this to evolve.

Current thinking (which we often do not hear much about) is asking the question, "Does Science Point to God?" In another book, *Is Atheism Dead?* Metaxas devotes one of the three parts of the book—eight chapters and over 100 pages—to address this situation.[8]

Do you see how John's Gospel today challenges the view that God does not exist, that this is all a random, evolutionary chance event?

People who are serious about science, about evidence, are once again staring at John's Gospel. It beautifully has stood up against various dominant world views through time. It will continue to do so.

When John wrote, "These things are written so that you might believe...," one of the things written was John 1:1-18. Praise God.

---

[1] Ibid, Wilkens.

[2] Celsius. *On the True Doctrine,* translated by R. Joseph Hoffman, (Oxford University Press, NY, 1987), p. 106.

[3] www.pbs.org/faithandreason/theogloss/logos-body.html, accessed April 30, 2022.

[4] John C. Lennox, *God and Stephen Hawking: Whose Design is it Anyway?* (Lion Books, Oxford, UK. 2011), p.11.

[5] History of the Big Bang Theory. en.wikipedia.org/wiki/History_of_the_Big_Bang_theory, accessed March 15, 2021.

[6] Einstein's Lost Theory Uncovered, February 24, 2014, www.scientificamerican.com/article/einsteins-lost-theory-uncovered/.

[7] Eric Metaxas, *Miracles* (Dutton. New York, NY. 2014), p. 36.

[8] Eric Metaxas, *Is Atheism Dead?* (Salem Books, Washington, D.C.), pp. 3-116.

APPENDIX

WAYS TO SHARE JESUS WITH OTHERS

All of this starts with "Read & Carry": remember to first be in the Word and second to ask God to lead you. With that said, let's get practical about sharing Jesus with others, what this method simply calls "Sharing." In all these examples, the Word of God, not Gospel Tracts, is being shared. Gospel Tracts are good, but they normally present a human point of view with the Word of God added. Here is a list of situations for sharing a pocket-sized Gospel of John from a myriad of life situations of what has been referred to as Personal Work:

- Ways as you go about your day
- Ways to speak with your family and friends
- Ways to share at work with people you are in regular contact with
- Ways to share at work with people you occasionally come into contact with.
- Ways to share as part of street evangelism
- Ways to share as part of a feeding ministry
- Ways to share as part of a sports ministry

- Ways, as a business owner, to share your faith
    - With your employees.
    - With your customers
    - With your suppliers
- Leadership considerations with specialized ministries

WAYS AS YOU GO ABOUT YOUR DAY

The challenge is twofold. First, how to offer the Gospel to someone. Second, what to say to the person.

Let's tackle the second question first. Here are some examples of what people say. What you say needs to be in your own words, but perhaps the examples below might get you started.

Examples of what to say: In increasing order of boldness of presenting the Gospel.

- I have a present for you.
- Can I give you this as a gift? I hope you might read it during a break in your day.
- I would like to give you this little book as a gift. Its message changed my life, and I simply wanted to share it. I hope you might read one chapter a day.
- What do you think about Jesus? (Wait for an answer such as, "I don't know?," "I don't like Christians," "I like him") and then ask, "Would you like to read what Jesus said in his own words for yourself?"

Examples of how to offer: In increasing order of boldness

- Simply leave it behind with a note
- After a friendly greeting (described above), hand it to the person and don't wait for a response.

- After a friendly greeting, offer to open it up and point out some specific verses or teaching.

- After a friendly greeting, offer to open it up, point out some specific verses, and offer to read it together with them (say a chapter at a time) and text or email back and forth.

- Do all of that and invite them to coffee or church.

- Not do any of the above, and simply invite them to coffee to chat about spiritual things or invite them to church.

Using the examples above, here are samples of the varied locations where people do this as they go about their day. You can engage the person to the various degrees described as God leads.

- Greet a parking lot attendant using one of the above ways next time you park your car in a lot. They usually have time and often nothing to read.

- If you find yourself in the hospital or doctor's office, using one of the above ways, greet your health care providers, patients, etc. during treatment. We receive many stories. The most humbling stories for me include ones from cancer patients as they receive chemotherapy.

- If you find yourself pulled over by the police, using one of the above ways, share a Gospel after the officer does their work. One person had a minor car accident. After all the necessary actions had taken place, they felt God's call to share with the person who caused the accident. The person who was hit gave the other person a Gospel as a gift. As you might expect, they were really surprised. It ministered to the person who caused the accident.

- When you find yourself in the bank, using one of the above ways, share a Gospel. Some people do it with a note to the bank teller. You need to be careful as often times, they will think it's a robbery note until they realize what it is!

- When you find yourself at a gas station, using one of the above ways, share a Gospel with others filling their cars at the same time.

- When you find yourself paying your bills, include the Gospel with a short note of encouragement. We have one member, a 94-year-old who can't leave her home, who continues to share their faith in this way.

- When you find yourself ordering food for delivery, using one of the above ways, share a Gospel with the person who delivers your food—don't forget an appropriate tip! We have folks who keep Gospels by their door, so they are ready. (They pray before they do it—God is not a gumball machine!)

- When you are in school, as a student, have a Gospel that you put on top of your books. People will notice and ask what it is. You can tell them it's a really cool little book you're reading. They might ask if they can read it too. Using this method, one high school student shared many, and students accepted Christ because of her faithfulness!

LET GOD SPEAK

At the end of the day, people value authenticity and recognize that your motivation is genuine love toward them.

WAYS TO SPEAK WITH YOUR FAMILY AND FRIENDS

Without a doubt, this is the toughest group of people to share your faith with. They know most of your foibles, and you know many of theirs. You have, as the saying goes, "history" with each other. You have installed each other's "buttons." Now, take all of that and add religion and faith, and as you know, it can all go awry rather quickly.

With a stranger, the challenge is what to say and exactly how to offer the Gospel. With family and friends, you need to have an approach or plan that fits the situation.

In a moment, I will address a few different situations, but first let me reinforce the need for prayer and the Lord's leading. Because we love our family and friends so much, because we so desire they know God, we charge in without ever praying and listening to God.

I suggest first you simply love and build a relationship with them. What does that look like? Let me ask a few questions. Do you know what their interests are? Do you know what job they have and the challenges of that job? Do you know what their hopes and dreams are? Do you know if they have health issues? How much time do you actually spend with them? All of this is to say, most of the time:

> *With family and friends, you need to earn the right to speak to them.*

I say "most of the time" because God is in charge. I have plenty of stories where God opened a door, a believing member of the family stepped through, and the Holy Spirit showed up. We need to be in tune with God.

You will need to overcome a few feelings and emotions. I expect they know you are a Christian. They may think you are weird. They may think you are a bigot.[1] They may not think any of these things, yet you might believe they do. It is hard. You need to put all that aside and be willing to be in their lives.

Let's look at three possible situations: they are hostile to you, you don't really know them, and finally, you have built a relationship with them.

Hostile to You

You need to ask permission to talk with them about God and/or faith, and you need to be willing to really invest the time to love them.

Let's say the relationship, for whatever reason, is one where the family or friend is really not interested in knowing you. What do you do? Answer: You ask permission to be in their lives. How?

I suggest the communication start with something like, "Hey, we're cousins, I know we are not terribly close, but I was wondering if we could get to know each other more?" You should not be surprised if the response is hostile. "Why, do you want to push your religion on me?" You might respond, "I want to get to know you. I won't talk about Jesus unless you ask. Following Jesus is how I am trying to "do my life." I simply want to get to know you."

Now think about the above dialog. Do you really want to get to know them, to love them? You need to answer that question as the starting point. It is why this needs to be led by God. I know people who have been in relationships for decades before the other person says, "Can you tell me about this Jesus stuff?" Is God leading you to a few decades of investment in this person?

They are not hostile, but you don't really know them.

Let's look at the next situation. *They are not hostile, but you don't really know them:* You need to let them get to know you and your faith. Don't lead with your faith. Lead with you, all of you.

Let's say you have made contact. The starting point of the relationship is not negative but more neutral. You each want to explore if you have common likes and interests. This dynamic will be especially true in new relationships, whether you've just married into a family or made some new friends.

So get started exploring. Find out what you each like to read, what movies you watch, and what music you listen to. I expect your choices will be full of Christian artists. That alone will get your family and friends' attention. *Wait for them to ask* why you like the things you like. Which is the question you might ask them, "Why do you like that author or music?" You should also have thought about your answers to questions you ask *ahead of time.* I am not asking you to be manipulative, but I know your heart. Your heart is to invite them to meet Jesus. So think about your answers ahead of time to avoid missteps. You don't need to have answers ahead of time for a million questions. I would suggest, however, that you have answers to the questions you ask them.

The way I approach this situation is first to be flexible and be ready. Flexible in that the person you are speaking with may be more extroverted and speak first, or they may wait for you. Ready in terms of knowing how you would answer the questions you are asking for yourself. For myself, I ready myself by sorting my answers into two broad categories. Here they are:

For music and movies, I would say something like, "I like things that are upbeat, things that affirm life, I know some of them might be corny, but there is so much negativity in the world that these build me up. I also like action-adventure movies. I am drawn to movies and books that capture the struggle between good and evil." Be willing to let them know the last movie you went to or the current music you are listening to.

For books (and again, this is me), I would say, "I am always interested in learning, so I read a lot of books about what I believe, about God, and about how to live my life." I will read some fiction just for a break. Let them know your favorite book and the ones you are currently reading. (David's favorite books (beyond the Bible) *Les Miserable* by Victor Hugo, *Dead Man Walking* by Sister Helen Prejean, *Blue Like Jazz* by Donald Miller, and any book on Leadership or Business Excellence because I need all the help I can get.)

Be ready to answer questions like, "What are you reading right now, or what movie are you hoping to see next?"

They may say, "Okay, let's go watch that movie together."

Your world will probably clash with theirs, and I don't think it matters too much whether you are talking with a family member or a friend. There may be movies they want you to watch and activities they want you to do that you may not be comfortable engaging with. May I suggest you don't do them? Look, in black and white theological terms, you are hanging out with unredeemed sinners. I know that is harsh, but true. I once heard Bishop Ed Salmon, former Episcopal Bishop of South Carolina and later Dean of Nashotah House Theological Seminary, say, with his rich Arkansas accent, "You can hang out with sinners. Jesus hung out with sinners, just make sure you know which way the power is flowin'!" When you go with them, which way will the power be flowing?

How do you decline attending a movie or some other activity? Look, you are trying to be friends. Friends don't have to agree on everything. Friends don't have to do everything together. You simply say you do not want to do what they are suggesting. If they press for why, simply say you do not enjoy it, or the activity is not good for you. If they continue to press, I would say, "Look, I like being your friend (or cousin, etc.), but please don't pressure me on this; it is just not good for me."

A good friend will, at some point, provide you an open door to talk about your faith. Your natural response will be to try and explain God and the Gospel. You will, therefore, immediately have put yourself (from your friend's point of view) in the expert seat. That means they will begin asking you many questions about God, the world, moral issues, political issues, etc. Don't fall into the trap of thinking you have to answer every question.

Here is where I suggest you let God do the heavy lifting.

You might say, "I believe Jesus is God. I believe he came to earth, lived, died, and actually rose again, for me! Following him has given me my best life. Understand, I mess up a lot, but I know God loves me. Can we just read this little book together? I promise I won't argue. I just want you to hear him in his own words. We can talk about what you think. After we read it, we can talk about all those hard questions. In the end, I hope I can still be your friend."

Then do it. Read the Gospel of John together. Ask questions to your friend like, "What would you think if you were with a man who really healed someone right before your eyes?" The Pocket Testament League at www.ptl.org has reading guides to help you with these questions.

You have a real relationship with them.

Let's turn to the third situation: *You have a real relationship with them*. In this case, you need to let them lead. You need to be ready to love them.

Much of what has been written earlier about building the relationship applies. Let's assume you know them or <u>had</u> known them for years. Perhaps they recently came back into your life. Perhaps you have known them for years and you have just accepted Jesus. The scenarios may vary, but what is the same is that you know each other. As the saying goes, "You have history together." Perhaps something has changed (like newfound faith on your part!). That change provides a window of opportunity.

I want to again suggest you pray and let God lead. Eventually, they will engage you, or you will just know it is the right time to engage them.

Let me use myself as an example. I came to faith late in life. I had all sorts of friendships and relationships in the corporate world at work. All those people were faced with me being different.

They noted I was different. They noticed I closed my door at lunch (I was reading my Bible). They were surprised when I apologized for saying something mean. They were thrilled I stopped cursing. And with all that, in hindsight, I could have done this much better.

When any of us first become a follower of Jesus, we are pretty jazzed up. We want to tell everyone. We should. We just need to think about how.

I would suggest returning to the above comment about not mistakenly getting yourself into the expert seat. Use the above Read—Carry—Share ® method, offer a Gospel of John, and let the Word of God do the heavy lifting of the human heart.

There is one other unique aspect you have with family and friends—very special moments in your life, big moments where you can share your faith. On these occasions, don't apologize for following Jesus. You don't need to hide your faith. Check out these poignant moments where people have used Gospels of John with their families.

- One couple, for their wedding, had Gospels of John as party favors at every table. They were tremendously gracious about this gift. During the toast, they noted that this was the happiest day of their lives, that they were praying that Jesus would guide their marriage, that they loved their family and friends, and they simply wanted to share Jesus. This was not a day to argue but a day to celebrate love. They hoped people would read the book, perhaps a chapter a day. They even offered to talk with people (but after the honeymoon). They then emphasized that today was a celebration, a party, not a church meeting, so let's celebrate. Their love for everyone showed.

- One person, for their birthday, had them for everyone. Similar to the wedding above, it was a party. The person celebrating their birthday shared some remarks. They thanked their family and friends for coming. They shared that their family and friends brought richness to their lives. They then said something like, "Look, I don't want to get too religious, but you all know that Jesus adds richness to my life. Jesus is hugely important to me. On this day, when you have all come to celebrate with me, I wanted to give you something. I ask you to read a chapter a day. I would be happy to talk to you more about it. Thanks so much for coming!"

- Many people have incorporated them into their funerals, or the funerals of loved ones. Consider, most of us, at some point, plan our funeral. Those plans are put into action by the funeral director, a family member, or another trusted person. We have people who share the Gospel of John as part of their service. They even have a personal message printed on the inside cover of every Gospel, a message they want to share. Some people may find this idea morbid. But pause and think about how, at your funeral, everyone is wondering where you are. You can tell them you are confident you are with Jesus. You can, by leaving God's Word, give them comfort by directing them to a certain chapter, such as John 14 or 15. It should be a part of the Gospel of John that the person planning the service feels drawn to share.

There are many other events—baptisms (this ought to be a no-brainer for offering people a Gospel), graduation, a party—when you are moving away from your friends for a new job or school. You can hand them out at a Superbowl party. The list goes on. Just be winsome!

---

[1] David Kinnaman & Gabe Lyons, *unChristian*, (Baker Books, 2012), p. 11.

WAYS TO SHARE AT WORK WITH PEOPLE YOU ARE IN *REGULAR* CONTACT WITH

We spend a great deal of time at work. Many of our relationships, even our friends, are through work. If you are close to your coworkers, then I suggest you refer to the earlier section. This section is for people you know, not deeply, yet you see them regularly, and God has put them in your life daily.

How do we share our faith? Can we share our faith, or will we get in trouble? Will sharing our faith somehow affect our professional working relationship? The list of questions is long. In this section, many of those questions are addressed.

To begin, the art of sharing your faith is a process. That is true for your family, your friends, and also those you work with. It is a process because it is about relationship building.

Part of the process is being genuine. What is the most common Monday morning question at work? Answer: "What did you do this weekend?" I would think it would be natural that among the few things you might list is, "…and we went to church." How about the ministry you are involved in? Let's say you go on a local, or even international, mission trip. I would think that would be something you would talk about. The point is that your faith is integrated into all aspects of your life, so simply share what is going on in your life.

Perhaps, as you are reading this section, you are thinking, "But I have kept that part of my life private from my coworkers." Don't worry; simply begin to introduce it into your conversation. You might even have a coworker say something like, "Wow, we've worked together for years and I did not know you went to church." A reaction like that is an open door for you to gently note that you do attend church, and you could share a little more with them.

The next part of the process regards how you handle life. In Matthew 5:45, Jesus says, "He sends rain on the just and the unjust." My point? You will face hardship in your life. Your kids will get sick. Your parents will age. Perhaps you or your spouse will face challenges even more difficult. People at work will possibly know when you face these challenges and how/if your faith buoyed you. Your behavior regards how you handle those life events will set the stage for talking about your faith. Your coworkers will face many of those same life challenges and might naturally ask your counsel.

Finally, do you do anything at work that demonstrates your faith? In one season, I read my Bible at lunch. I was a manager. I had an office and an assistant. I would close my door for 30 minutes and read my Bible. It was one of the rare times my door was closed. One day I heard my assistant stop someone from entering my office. This person asserted they had to see me. My assistant and this person had an exchange that I could hear. He was pressing to enter my office. Ultimately, she said, "Look, you can barge in there, but let me tell you, our afternoons are much better when he has these 30 minutes, and yours probably will be too!"

That took place when I was a plant manager of a nuclear power plant. We were refueling it. On many afternoons I was, let's say, "not the best version of myself." It was a hard job with many demands but also a new season for me. I was barely a new Christian. I started that job as a non-Christian and became one in the middle. I never stood up and made any big announcement. However, people noticed a few things. They noticed my office door closed at lunch. They noticed a Bible. I started this routine very soon after coming to faith.

People were used to me being demanding and many times unreasonable. All the old parts of me had not died. People watched me wrestle. They saw me trying to follow Jesus. I expect they were wondering if God could really love a knucklehead like me. I expect they were wondering if God could change me.

Perhaps your job is demanding and stressful. Perhaps you have an unreasonable boss. Perhaps you are the boss. Our words and actions will set the stage. Our words and actions will determine if we will be able to share the Gospel effectively.

To be clear, I am not talking about being the perfect Christian. It is not about perfection but about a bit of transparency. How much transparency is something to pray about; let God lead you. Depending on where you work, and who you work with, you need to use judgment. In the end though, it is about letting people see how God is walking with you in your life.

You also need to be sensitive to the hierarchy of your organization and the position you fill in the company. For example, if you are a supervisor, then you naturally have positional power over others. Be careful; people may misunderstand and think they have to become a Christian in order to keep their job or get a raise. That would be wrong. In my own situation, someone very senior to me arranged for another person less senior to mentor me. They were thrilled I came to believe in Jesus; they wanted to jump in and help, but they knew the office dynamics warranted something different.

Regardless, people are looking for support, advice, and someone to simply talk to who won't turn it into gossip. If people see you as a person who is like that, then you will be a magnet. You will naturally be in a position to share your faith.

Let me offer some phrases people use for sharing their faith and a Gospel of John.

Examples of what to say: In increasing order of boldness.

- When people ask you about how you are living life, simply say, "I am simply trying to follow Jesus. His way is what I have found best for my life. I don't get it right all the time, but his way is the best. Can I give you this gift? It is about Jesus. It tells of his life. It shows me how to follow him. It is filled with his own words."

- You might add to the end of the above, "I would be happy to read it together with you. We could read a chapter at a time. I promise not to lecture." (Resources exist to help guide the reading for a new seeker, such as the 21 Day Challenge from The Pocket Testament League at www.ptl.org)

- Another answer you may offer when people inquire about your life is, "The message of this book changed my life. I would like to give it to you as a gift." Again, you can include an invitation to read together or even to attend church with you.

- Another approach is to first ask questions. Perhaps people see a Bible at your workplace or note you mention going to church. They might come up to you and say something like, "You go to church?" or "Where do you go to church?" I suggest asking a question as you answer. You might say, "I do; what do you think about Jesus? (Wait for the answer such as, "I don't know," "I don't like Christians," "I like him"). Based on their answer, you might agree. They might say, "I did go to a church, but the pastor (or the people) really hurt me." You would respond from your own point of view but let me suggest you not defend the church or pastor or people. If appropriate, you might even say, "Yeah, I get it; that happened to me. It was hard for me. I kept confusing Jesus with the people at church who had hurt me." And then ask, "Would you like to simply read about Jesus? We could read it together."

- Maybe you have been talking to someone about faith for years. Remember, it is about loving them first. Yes, you want them to meet Jesus, but if that becomes your singular motivation, then you won't give them the space and time they need. For example, in one of my relationships at work, for years, I was answering questions about the church and the Bible with a coworker/friend. I felt like our relationship had devolved to "he would ask a theological question. I would give an answer." One day in exasperation, I said to him, "Look, you can ask me all the questions you want; I will try and answer, but two points. First, I don't have all the answers. Second, I will still be your friend even if you don't accept Jesus. Can we talk about other stuff!" We were in a car and he was driving. He almost drove off the road. He thought my sole interest was converting him to my way of thinking, and so he actually had dug his heels in.

WAYS TO SHARE AT WORK WITH PEOPLE YOU *OCCASIONALLY COME* IN CONTACT WITH

The previous section discussed ways to share your faith with people who you have regular, even frequent, contact with. They know when you or a member of your family is sick. They know when a family member or friend passes away. They have a sense of the rhythm of your life. You have a sense of these rhythms in theirs.

This section seeks to discuss ways you can share your faith at work with people you occasionally come in contact with. People who know your name but don't know all about you.

You may be an employee of a firm or an independent contractor (If you own your own business, then later sections seek to speak to that situation.)

Regardless of whether you are an employee or contractor, the way you share the Gospel really comes down to your local setting. Your sharing is typically less about whether you do or do not share and more about the degree of sharing you do.

You need to understand what the company you work for or are under contract with expects. Our witness for Jesus starts with how those who have hired us see us. Imagine if your behavior makes your employer worried that your zeal for your faith might actually hurt the company. That would not be a good witness.

That does not mean you need to be silent.

We have people who often use the methods and techniques described in the first section, "Ways as you go about your day." They customize their opening line to match their line of work. What they are doing is using the opportunity of their work to come into contact with people.

For some folks, your job will bring you into contact with people for short moments of time, but those moments will happen over and over (the person who orders coffee from you so regularly, you know how they take their coffee). That is just one example of how the Lord puts the same people routinely in your path. You will see them on some of their "good days" and "not-so-good days."

Again, don't treat people like gumball machines. Use the Read—Carry—Share ® method. By design, it has you daily in God's Word and daily in prayer. Pray, "Lord, every day I bump into 'Bill,' show me if this is the day to reach out to him. Give me the words."

Here Are Some Common Situations

Construction, Shipyard, and folks on big office projects are often part of a small team but also meet many people during their day. Many of them share a Gospel of John with their teammates based on the discussion above (ways to share at work with people you are in *regular* contact with.) They also share with the many people they regularly come in contact with. They often know the other person's name. As the Lord leads, they simply offer a Gospel with words of encouragement. Here are some examples.

- Sales Representatives travel regularly to the same clients. They know the people they meet by name, but not intimately. There is always time for small talk. They share a Gospel with them. Not on their first sales call, but after a few. They share a message such as, "I know it will be a few months until we see each other again, but I wanted to share this book with you. Its message changed my life. One representative has given out over 50, and no one has refused to take one! Another offers to read it together and email back-and-forth between sales calls and receives positive responses.

- Other Sale Representatives put a Gospel in the orders they deliver. This, of course, depends on your company, but many folks who have permission or autonomy share Gospels of John and have great relationships with their customers.

- Nurses and others in health care are special people. God has given them hearts of compassion. We have many nurses and health care workers who share. Their compassion makes them very good at building rapport with people quickly. They pray a lot before they share. They never put Gospel sharing over their primary responsibility. But at the right time, they share God's Word with people who are hurting and in need -- both patients and their families. Here is an example of what they say, "I know it is hard right now, and you are going through so much. I want to leave this little book with you to read. I pray it will give you comfort." Every year The Pocket Testament League receives many stories from professionals in the health care industry who do this exactly.

- Truck drivers and delivery folks from all over the nation give a Gospel when they drop something off. Some of them have the same route, and they know the people. Some don't know the people.

Regardless, again with simple words of encouragement, they offer a Gospel.

- Bus drivers, Uber/Lyft drivers, and taxi drivers encounter hundreds of people. Many not having a good day. Gospel-giving drivers pay attention to those stepping aboard. They offer them to passengers they speak with and who show interest. For example, if the person expresses they are having a bad day, one driver says, "Looks like you are having a hard day. Can I give you this book to help lift your spirits? It is my gift to you."

- Another technique Uber, Lyft, and Taxi drivers use is to have a stack of Gospels on display. Many cars have bucket seats with a console. These drivers often have bottled water to offer and a display of a Gospel with a catchy cover. As the conversation develops, people often ask, "What is this little book?" They then, based on how the conversation is going, talk about their faith, or simply say, "I love that book; it changed my life. It is my gift to you!"

- Cleaning people are in homes and rooms. Those who clean other folks' homes often have a firsthand view of the other person's challenges. They offer a Gospel in love at the right time—the right time being when the Holy Spirit leads them after they have prayed. Other folks who clean never see the people they are serving; they simply leave a Gospel in each room or on each bed for the person when they arrive. We have one story where a man took the Gospel, read it a few days later, accepted Christ, and drove back to find the person who left the Gospel and thanked them!

- Service technicians for phone, plumbing, electrical, carpentry, cable TV, etc., have great opportunities to talk with people. Most of them wait until after they have done the job the person asked them to do. Then, based on the Lord's leading, and how much their customer wants to talk, they find an opportunity to share. Some simply say as they are leaving, "It was my privilege to serve you today. I want to give you this book as a gift; I hope you might read one chapter a day."

As already discussed, we have people who often use the methods and techniques described in the first section, "Ways as you go about your day." They customize their opening line to match their line of work.

All these examples come from real people who use the Read—Carry—Share ® method. You can read their stories sent to The Pocket Testament League at www.ptl.org/stories.

What they are doing is using the opportunity of their work to come into contact with people. Again, they don't treat people like gumball machines. They spend time in God's Word, and they pray that the Lord puts people in their path as they place a Gospel of John in their pocket or purse.

WAYS TO SHARE AS PART OF STREET EVANGELISM

Street evangelists: I love them! They are so bold. They are so creative. They are so fearless. They are this way because they love Jesus, and they have a heart for people in all sorts of situations that they find as they go out "into the streets." They want to connect people to Jesus, many of whom are separated from God and His Love.

Before we list specific examples, just a few principles.

- If you believe God's Word has power, and if you believe the Holy Spirit does the work, our observation is the best evangelists witness love, not judgment.

- If you believe God's Word has power, then you invite versus argue.

- If you believe God's Word has power, then you pray versus debate. Literally ask the person in front of you if you can pray for them right then and there.

I am not saying be a wimp. I am saying be a positive witness. Share God's truth in a non-judgmental way. In the first section, "Ways as you go about your day," I listed a number of phrases. You can use many of those and more. Below are real-life reports that can serve as examples. You will see people in specific contexts, and you will see more examples of the phrases they use to introduce the Gospel of John.

Here are some examples:

- One young woman, amid the many tarot card readers, psychics, and other promoters of false beliefs, sets up a table on Venice Beach each week offering the Gospel of John. People ask her, "What are you offering?" Wow! What an open door. Remember, this is a moment of invitation. The Gospel is the source of true, lasting hope.

- High school groups set up tables in the middle of all sorts of village/town/city events with a sign that asks, "Need Prayer?" Often this is in the midst of many artists, psychics, fortune tellers, etc. Many people stop to pour out their hearts.

- College groups have a table in their quad to answer questions. They offer the Gospels there to whoever would like one and, depending on the conversation, invite people to small groups.

- Students go out on Sunday with donuts and offer the donuts to people along with the Gospels. They then sit and talk with them.

WAYS TO SHARE AS PART OF A FEEDING MINISTRY

Works of mercy to others is a huge part of living out our faith. Consider this scene from Matthew 25:35-40. Jesus is talking about people entering heaven.

> "For I was hungry and you gave me food to eat. I was thirsty and you gave me drink. I was a stranger and you took me in. I was naked and you clothed me. I was sick and you visited me. I was in prison and you came to me."
>
> Then the righteous will answer him, saying, "Lord, when did we see you hungry and feed you, or thirsty and give you a drink? When did we see you as a stranger and take you in, or naked and clothe you? When did we see you sick or in prison and come to you?" The King will answer them, "Most certainly I tell you, because you did it to one of the least of these my brothers, you did it to me."

Many who seek to minister to people who lack food and reach them for Jesus note that we need to be sensitive to the specific situations of the people being served. Folks in need are dealing with any number of issues, and we must not presume we know their situation. This concern for each individual's circumstances means we should first tend to the physical need of their hunger. If people are starving, their hunger is real, and God's people should not only have something to say about it but be doing something about it first. It is hard to hear the Gospel if you're hungry.

In outreach ministries of mercy, justice, etc., one image used is the Cross. The vertical arm of the Cross symbolizes our need to present the eternal dimension of their need for Christ. The horizontal arm represents those real physical needs, needs that if we care about them as people, we will work to meet.

The first step for any of these ministries is to explicitly identify that they want to present the Gospel, not only with deeds of mercy but also by intentionally presenting the Gospel in words.

This is not a small decision. At times I find wonderful people, doing amazing work, who do not want to give voice to the Gospel. They don't want to mention Jesus. They don't want to talk about sin and the need for a savior. They don't want to even share a pamphlet or booklet. Jesus' name is absent. I get it. They don't feel like they are Billy Graham or D.L. Moody. They perhaps are concerned that people will think the service they are offering is contingent upon them believing in Jesus.

Here is where all that this book has been suggesting comes to a point. When doing works of mercy, I want to suggest that God be explicitly included. You can do this, and you don't have to be Billy Graham. You can simply offer a Gospel of John; you can let God's Word do the heavy lifting. Isn't that thought freeing? Below are ways different feeding ministries do exactly that.

- Some ministries, like food banks, simply put a Gospel of John in every food box.

- Other ministries put a Gospel of John in a food box with a short greeting of love and with a few pointing those that receive the box to a specific story of Jesus feeding the 5,000.

- Still others, when they deliver the food in person, tell them there is a Gospel of John inside the box.

- Still others, when they deliver the food in person, as they drop off the box, open the box and go through what is inside, providing instructions for food preparation, and sharing there is a Gospel of John.

- Still others, when they deliver the food in person, drop off the box, open the box and go through what is inside, providing instructions for food preparation, share that the reason they provide food is because they are trying to show God's love to people, and there is a Gospel of John.

- Still others, when they deliver the food in person, drop off the box, open the box and go through what is inside, providing instructions for food preparation, share that the reason they provide food is because they are trying to show God's love to people, open the Gospel of John, and read one of the stories.

- Still others, do all that and invite them to church.

For the examples where you are speaking, keep it simple. Say something like, "I wanted to also share this Gospel of John with you. It has given me such hope when I have faced trouble." Or "We wanted to also share this Gospel of John with you. It has given me such hope when I have faced trouble. I want you to know Jesus really loves you. You can read all about him."

I pray you can see that there are different degrees of offering a person Gospels of John, from simply putting a Gospel in a food box, all the way up to speaking with those being served and inviting them to join you in church. Regardless, all involve offering them the Living Word of God in love.

WAYS TO SHARE AS PART OF A SPORTS MINISTRY

We love our sports. It does not matter what age. We start our kids young. The need for cultural sensitivity has already been noted. Sports can cut through cultural divides. Trying to get a round ball into a goal breaks down many a barrier.

Many great organizations use sports as a way to build into people's lives. Here are just two examples.

Some ministries include organizing sports camps and leagues; many of these ministries are in underprivileged areas and invest in people's lives. This investment includes sharing the Good News.

Other organizations bring athletic celebrities to people to share their faith. Many of these highly successful individuals share either the tough circumstances they escaped from, the emptiness of worldly success, or both. They share the challenge that someday the spotlight will fade. They tell of Jesus, who rescued them.

People use sports in many ways to share the Gospel. What follows are examples of how a Gospel of John has been integrated into various sports ministries. As you review the different ways, some will be appropriate for settings that might be in public schools, and others only appropriate for groups where the method has been made clear ahead of time.

- Some will do a sort of "coach talk" at the end of practice, making a point about life and referring to a specific episode or verse in the Gospel of John. After doing this a number of times, they will hand out the Gospels.

- Some require (you read correctly—require) reading a chapter of the Gospel to play. The practice or game starts first with a Bible Study on the chapter. They all open it up, it is read, and they talk about the chapter. This really does not take that long. The remarkable thing is that non-believers of all ages actually respect this discipline.

- One ministry rewards the kids if they come to a certain number of practices and complete the Bible Study (reading John's Gospel), such as taking them on a mission trip.

For those that have a person share a testimonial, the Gospel is woven into their talk to various degrees. There are many ways to do this, here are just a few.

- When everyone arrives, they are given a few items, including a pocket-size Gospel of John*.

- When everyone arrives, they are given a few items, including a pocket-size Gospel of John*. During the talk, maybe several times, as the athlete is telling their story, they will tell people to open up their Gospels, go to a certain page and look at a verse. The celebrity will then connect that verse specifically to a powerful moment in their lives. At the end of the talk, everyone is encouraged to read the entire Gospel.

*I met one director of a great athletic ministry who shared with me how he pulled entire full Bibles out of the garbage after an event; most were covered in ketchup from the lunch they served. He was heartbroken. He knew how much the Bibles cost and how hard it was to raise the funds. I listened.

He asked me what I thought. I said, "I have three thoughts. First is the Parable of the Sower: some seed falls on the hard path. It is a reality. Second, if you were not upset, it means you really don't care about the people you are trying to reach or the donors who support the ministry. I am glad you care. Third, I know some of our pocket-sized Gospels end up with ketchup on them. I take heart that they cost much less to produce, and so we are being good stewards. Further, for those who don't throw them away, who read them, when it takes root, it is a great time to provide them an entire Bible."

Many sports ministries (and others) tell us how they love the Gospel of John because it sorts out people who want to go further. They describe how people come to them after having read the Gospel of John and want more. Those individuals are on fire for Jesus and willingly receive an entire Bible!

WAYS AS A BUSINESS OWNER TO SHARE YOUR FAITH

As a business owner, you face a number of challenges. You wonder if you should share the Gospel. You wonder if you legally can share the Gospel. You wonder if it will hurt your business if you do share the Gospel. You tell yourself that as a Christian business owner, you provide jobs with good benefits, and you run a business with integrity. You use the profits of your business to bless your employees and all sorts of ministries. You wonder, will sharing hurt all of that good stuff? You might ask, "Am I not doing enough?"

Those questions, and many more, are valid. There are wonderful organizations that serve businesses, that help business owners and CEOs sort out how to see their business as a ministry.[1] To be clear, many ministry opportunities exist for business. The next three sections are focused on sharing the Gospel with three segments you come into contact with: employees, customers, and vendors.

But first, business leaders often ask if they can legally share the Gospel with their employees. Here is what Alliance Defending Freedom, the world's largest legal organization committed to protecting religious freedom, free speech, marriage and family, parental rights, and the sanctity of life, says:

> Employers may share their religious beliefs with their employees if the employees know that their continued employment, benefits, and advancement

within the company are not adversely affected by their rejection of the employer's religious beliefs. Likewise, employees who agree with their employer's religious beliefs cannot be preferentially treated because of their agreement with those beliefs.

Specifically, employers may share religious materials, such as pocket testaments, pamphlets, books, and newsletters, with their employees. Employers must be careful, however, not to take any adverse employment action against an employee or give employees the impression that they must agree with the employer's religious beliefs in order to keep their job, get a promotion, or retain their benefits.

In order to counter any impression that job security, benefits, and advancement are contingent upon faith, it is recommended that the religious materials state within the publication or in the area where the materials are provided that the employer does not discriminate on the basis of religion for purposes of continued employment, benefits or promotion.[2]

With this now clarified, let's examine your different mission fields.

Ways as a Business Owner to Share with Your Employees

Talent: we are all competing for it. Few businesses succeed with poor employees. Many companies recognize the critical nature of their team and have remarkable programs to serve and develop their people.

Would sharing the Gospel be one?

There are at least two reasons to share the Gospel with your employees.

First, if you love them, you will want them to meet Jesus. After all, they are not your people first; they are God's. You might even say God has brought these people into your life and into your company. If God has done this, then the question is, "For what purpose did God bring these specific people to my company?"

The second reason has to do with your company and its need for talent. The word I use in this regard is <u>transparency</u>. Imagine you spend the money to find the best person for a specific job. It involved hours of writing job descriptions, sifting through applicants, and narrowing the field down to a handful of qualified candidates. You carefully crafted questions. You prayed for God's guidance. After all that, you made your decision. You onboarded the person. As expected, it took time for them to get the feel of the position and company: weeks, maybe months.

And then it happens. They find out you are a Christian. Perhaps you are surprised that they are surprised. Perhaps you thought your faith would have been obvious. You are trying to run your company in accordance with Christian principles. For some reason, they missed the part where you are a Christian. They don't know much about Christianity, but perhaps what they know makes them suspicious.[3] No one has ever talked to them about you and your company trying to run it as a Christian company. They are confused. All they know about Christianity comes from the media, and that is very negative. They think maybe it isn't safe to ask about it. Maybe they will keep their head down. Maybe they are sitting at their desk wondering if they should leave. Either way, when an employee is wondering about any aspect of where they work, you've lost a degree of their commitment to your mission.

This is why many companies will actually include a Gospel of John in the application package. You might be shocked. Let's unpack this a bit.

The Gospel they offer has on the inside a personal note from the CEO. It says something like, "This book is being shared so you know what we are trying to do. We are trying to run a great company by following the teaching of Jesus. It is hard. We don't get it right all the time. We are sharing this book so you are not surprised. We will never force you to believe what we believe. We follow all the laws regarding hiring, promotion, etc. We are simply trying to be transparent."

Now imagine the impact that has on potential hires. They are looking at your company based on your product, your reputation, your salary, your benefits package, and the work you are offering them. You need to be making a compelling offer. It's been reported that this approach has actually created a positive openness with candidates. It also creates a workplace where the people at the top have said from the start, "We are trying. We don't get it right all the time."

Some companies don't do it at the application stage; they do it later. Often during onboarding as they explain the range of benefits and optional activities. Many non-Christian companies have clubs, softball teams, and teams that go to schools and mentor. The list is long. Christian companies have those and more. They might have Bibles and Gospels in a reading room. They might have ways for people to request prayer. They might offer Bible Studies at lunch. All is, of course, non-mandatory. All have nothing to do with employment or promotions or salary.

Unlike other sections in this book which gave a long list of examples of how to share, for a CEO, it is really about making the decision to do so. With that decision, then you put in place mechanisms that are both legal and support your company culture.

Your employees will understand you are a person of faith. They may even seek you out. You may find opportunities. Yet in this setting, it is less about you walking around handing out Gospels and more about you communicating your company's culture through your processes and programs—the processes and programs every company has. It gives the people committed to your charge a bit of space while at the same time letting them know who you are following.

Ways as a Business Owner to Share with Your Customers

If finding good talent is a challenge, how about the challenge of finding and keeping great customers!

We court our customers. We cajole our customers. We cater to our customers. Dare we touch the third rail (discussing politics or religion) with them?

Christian business owners have found through the years that the answer is a clear and profound YES! Remember, it starts with business owners being in the Word of God, and prayer.

Here is a revelation. Customers are people! They have lives like you and me. Those lives are filled with ups and downs. The simple "code to crack" is that you find a method of sharing the Gospel that communicates to your customers that your offer of the Gospel is completely not about you and all about your genuine concern for them.

Now to be clear, it is a bit "about you." You as a business owner have decided to take the risk and share the Gospel. That act alone will communicate something about you. If, however, you are doing it with the right motives and are guided by prayer, and if you really care about them as a person, then they will receive the Gospel (wondering about you for a brief moment) and begin thinking about how it intersects with their lives.

How you do it falls into two broad categories. Are you engaging large numbers of customers with your product or service? Or are your products and services concentrated with a relatively small number of clients?

Let's start with the large-scale numbers. You generally won't be interacting individually with your customers, so here, getting your message to them generally comes in the form of a hand-crafted message. The message is consistent with your brand and culture. Here are some ways that companies currently share the Gospel. The Pocket Testament League has stories of people accepting Christ from ALL these methods.

- Car dealers place Gospels in the standard information kit when the car is purchased or in the glove compartment.

- Companies that ship products always include a Gospel as part of their shipping insert, often times with a way to engage the CEO of the company sending the products.

- Companies that provide broad services include a Gospel with their material, often times with a way to engage the CEO.

- Companies have their receptionists, when they offer coffee or water to people who have come for an appointment, share a package of material about the company, which includes a Gospel.

- Companies have them prominently in their waiting areas, conference rooms, and board rooms frequented by customers. Often, they are part and parcel with the companies' vision and values displays.

Companies that offer products and services in a more individualized way will often interact with their clients differently than those described above. Therefore, how they share a Gospel of John is often different.

- Companies that offer legal, accounting, consulting, etc. often include a Gospel as part of their initial meeting and introductory briefing. This is often personalized with a way to connect with the CEO. (The transparency discussion offered regarding employees completely applies here.)

- Companies that install custom home systems (e.g., lighting and sound systems, new heating and cooling, etc.) often, at the end of the meeting where they teach the homeowner how to operate it, share a Gospel.

- Companies have their receptionists, when they offer coffee or water to people who have come for an appointment, share a package of material about the company, which includes a Gospel.

- Companies have them prominently in their waiting areas, conference rooms, and board rooms frequented by customers. Often, they are part and parcel with the companies' vision and values displays.

Ways as a Business Owner to Share with Your Suppliers

On top of finding great talent and going deeper with your customers, your suppliers play an integral role in you delivering top quality products and services. You, or members of your team, spent energy in contract negotiations around price, schedule, and quality standards.

These reasons, and more, point out that you are beginning to form, or have formed, a real relationship with them. That relationship is an opportunity to share your faith via a Gospel with them. Just like sharing your faith with your employees and customers, this transparency can help strengthen this critical connection.

Dealing with B2B, as it were, presents unique opportunities. The CEO on the other end of the phone knows many of the challenges and pressures you face. Therefore, when you step out in faith and share a Gospel, they will sit up and take notice. Here is one such story that I personally witnessed.

The CEO of a company, on its anniversary, sent a letter to some of their key suppliers. They make sophisticated, tight tolerance equipment. Their suppliers will make – or – break their performance. The letter included an offer to provide a lunch to the supplier's employees and a Gospel for each employee. The CEO in the letter explained that the success of the company was tightly connected to this supplier. As they reflected and celebrated on their anniversary, they wanted to bless those who had made all those years of success possible. The CEO who received the letter was blown away. He, too, was a Christian but had never thought about sharing his faith in the workplace. The multiple fruit from this event continues even today.

It goes beyond CEO to CEO. You can "bake a Gospel" into many processes, from sales calls to people dropping off supplies at your loading dock. Let's look at two such processes.

- A sales call to you or your company from one of your suppliers (or potential suppliers) presents the opportunity for that sales representative to get to know your company. Let's be real, if they are any good at sales, they will <u>want</u> to get to know your company: who you are. Their service or product will need to compete on price, schedule, and performance—and no doubt these will be the basis for your decision. Yet you still have an opportunity with the salesperson to demonstrate that you care about them by offering them a Gospel of John.

- The Loading Dock is a place where you might find the culture of your company. It can be hot. It can be cold. It is often forgotten about. Imagine this scene. It is a hot day. The truck pulls up, and you are just one stop of many for the driver. Then he is surprised by a cool bottle of water and a Gospel. What did he or she just learn about your company? That your company cares.

- And there is another side benefit. You can have your employees hand out a standard "package." Whether it is when they enter the lobby, to a sales presentation, to receiving goods on the loading dock. They don't have to "give a Gospel presentation." They merely need to deliver the message from the CEO. It is completely legal. Imagine the impact there!

- People have found many ways to incorporate sharing the Gospel. They display it prominently around their facilities. They include it when they pay their invoices. They include it when they send their invoices. They share it during company events. They make sure their chaplains have it.

Summary Thoughts Regarding Business Owners Sharing Their Faith

It's personal. It's personal for me. I was at the then peak of my career, managing a nuclear power plant, and my personal life was in shambles. A coworker shared his faith and led me to Christ. Please hear this loud and clear: I met Jesus in the workplace.

But it did not stop there. I needed discipling. My company president got engaged. I was several levels removed from him in a company of more than 2,500 people. But he knew. He knew I had accepted Jesus. He engaged me through a mid-level manager and sent me books to read, such as C.S. Lewis' *Mere Christianity* and Stuart and Fee's *How to Read the Bible for All It's Worth*. I was invited to go on retreats. Today I lead an organization that encourages millions of people to share their faith, in large part because people where I worked years ago were courageous enough to share Jesus with me.

If you are a business owner, I want to encourage you to share the Gospel.

---

[1] Five such organizations are C12 (www.joinc12.com), Convene (www.convenenow.com), FCCI (www.fcci.org), CBMC (www.cbmc.com), and CBMC International (www.cbmcint.com).

[2] Pruitt, Bob. "Sharing Gospels of John." email to David Collum, August 12, 2022.

[3] Ibid, Kinnaman, p. 11.

LEADERSHIP CONSIDERATIONS WITH SPECIALIZED MINISTRIES

Military, Veteran, College, Seniors, Prison, Addiction Recovery, Homeless, Etc.

When I meet leaders in these ministries, I am humbled. They have a passion, a drive for a specific group of people that is hard to describe. They often have personal experience. Jesus delivered them and freed them from the grasp of death.

Therefore, they are the experts. This section won't unpack the myriad of unique challenges these specialized ministries face. However, these experts often struggle with what every follower of Jesus struggles with. They ask, "How do I share the Gospel with a person who has been so beaten up by the world? What do I say? When do I say it?"

Sometimes, because they are so passionate about their calling and because they know the answer is found in Jesus, this struggle can be a real burden.

The Good News is that God's Word has power. The other good news is that there are many best practices for how to share a Gospel in these highly specialized settings.

I won't pretend to know the specific challenges each of these groups face. Therefore, I won't offer comments about their very specific contexts. I will, however, return to the main point of this book:

There is power in the Word of God. Let's use it.
Let's elevate God's Word back into the mix.

The key in each of these specialized settings seems to lie in the counselors and volunteers who are serving those in need. They are in tune with what is going on in each person's life. Therefore, the challenge lays first in the hand that is offering God's Word to the person in front of them.

If you are reading this and a follower of Jesus who loves Him, loves God's Word, and has a heart to see people saved, then I expect you will personally appreciate this idea of using a Gospel of John. If you lead a ministry, then you need to make sure your counselors and volunteers similarly appreciate the idea of introducing the Gospel to those being served. Let's unpack that a bit. What follows is what I have learned from these ministry leaders.

These specialized ministries draw volunteers from all walks of life. These ministries depend on these volunteers. Perhaps all these volunteers don't have the same passion you, the ministry leader, has to share Jesus. What do you do?

First you, as the leader, need to clarify your mission and method. Is the organization you are leading aiming to lead people to Christ <u>and</u> deal with their infirmity, or are you there to deal only or mostly with their infirmity, and perhaps if the opportunity presents itself, share the Good News?

Both ministries are great, but do you see the difference?

There is a big difference. The first ministry will lead much more with God. They will speak to the person about how they are created in the image of God. They will share how God loves them. How God is present with them in their suffering. This approach then naturally flows to the sharing of God's Word.

The second ministry will welcome the person and love them (sometimes it is tough love). There won't be talk of God. There will be serving their specific need. If the opportunity presents itself for a spiritual conversation, they respond. How might such an opportunity present itself? Several ways. The person receiving the help might ask, "Why is God doing this to me?" or "Where is God?" or "Why are you helping me?" Ministries are trained that when these questions arise, they are prepared to share a Gospel.

In either case, you will need to train your volunteers. This training is a mission field unto itself. Picture the scene. You hold the training to share a Gospel of John. You develop helpful catch-phrases as conversation starters. You have ready follow-on resources specific to the area you are serving. Yet with all that, you face a skeptical group. As you address the skepticism, you are ministering and discipling others.

Be sure to pray. Pray that God shows the power of His word to your volunteers. Remember my own story as I first came to The Pocket Testament League? God will hear your prayer, and now your volunteers will not only catch your vision but have a deeper relationship with the Lord.

Made in the USA
Middletown, DE
14 October 2024